NOSTRADAMUS

NOSTRADAMUS

His Life and Predictions

SUSAN CAPEL

With illustrations by Dario Poli

STUDIO
EDITIONS

First published in 1995 by Studio Editions Ltd,
Princess House, 50 Eastcastle Street,
London W1N 7AP

Frontispiece: 'The Alchemist' by Thomas Wijck.
Above: Engraving of Nostradamus.

Picture research by Julia Hanson
Designed by AB3 Design, London

Printed & bound by ORIENTAL PRESS, (DUBAI).

ISBN 1 85891 295 4

Extract on page 90 has been reproduced by
permission of Hamish Hamilton Ltd, from page
66 of *The Italians* by Luigi Barzini (London,
1964), copyright © 1964 Luigi Barzini.

Extract on page 127 has been reproduced by
permission of HarperCollins Publishers, Inc.,
from pages 120-121 of *Nectar in a Sieve* by
Kamala Markandaya, copyright © 1954 by
Harper & Row Publishers, Inc.

CONTENTS

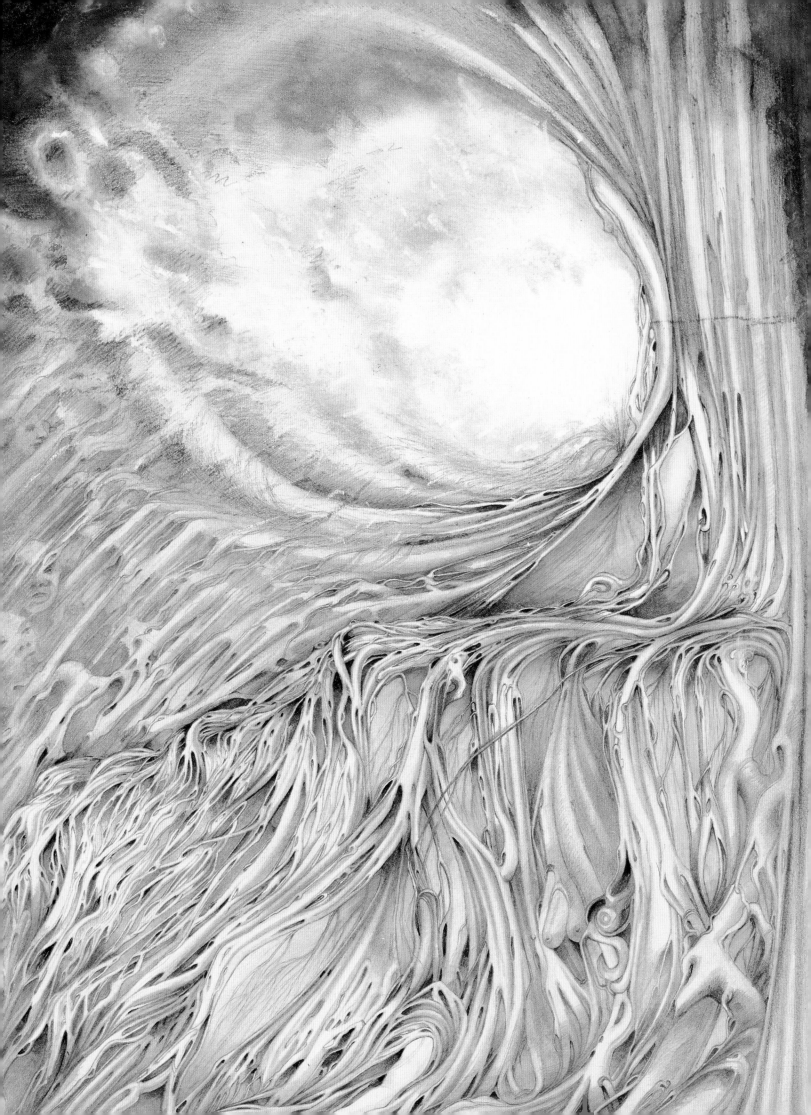

INTRODUCTION
THE LIFE AND WORKS OF NOSTRADAMUS

NOSTRADAMUS, THE GREAT sixteenth-century prophet whose vision encompasses the destiny of the whole world, is of enduring interest to people all over the planet. It is rare to hear him dismissed as an individual with no real relevance to our times. Despite his detractors (there are those who do not believe in prophetic communication and the deliberate obscurity of his predictions makes a definitive interpretation of his work difficult), Nostradamus's reputation as a prophet, nearly five hundred years after his birth in Provence, is even more vibrant today than it was following the first successful publication of the *Centuries* in 1555.

There are several reasons for his continuing fame. He was almost certainly in the right place at the right time. The French Queen, Catherine de Medici, was fascinated by anything to do with the occult and her interest in him brought his name to a wide audience. His place at the French court more or less guaranteed that his reputation would spread outside his native land. It reached England through one of Elizabeth I's ambassadors, Andrew Throckmorton, who advised his sovereign that Catherine quoted Nostradamus with as confident an air as if she had quoted St John or St Luke. That can hardly have endeared Catherine or Nostradamus to the Church authorities and the officers of the Inquisition, but – in the sixteenth century at least – there was little the

Church could do to the monarch or, presumably, to the monarch's protégé. Given the determination of the Inquisition to root out those whose thoughts and deeds were contrary to the teachings of the Church, it is difficult to see how else Nostradamus escaped a charge of heresy.

He was born at an exciting time. The spirit of the Renaissance – the European intellectual and cultural movement of the fourteenth to sixteenth centuries – permeated many walks of life. The revival of interest in classical art, literature and culture brought forgotten and discredited theories on the nature of the universe and the place of humans within it to life for new generations. Humanism – the concept of

Opposite page: 'Into Another Dimension'. Dario Poli's vision of mankind's inevitable struggle between the earthbound desires of its own materialistic nature and its spiritual striving toward the tunnel of pure light.

Below: People accused of heresy by the Inquisition are burnt at the stake. The Inquisition was established in 1231 by Pope Gregory IX to detect and punish heretics.

Above: Two alchemist's assistants at work, from a seventeenth century English manuscript. One stokes the furnace while the other arranges the apparatus.

them forbidden by the Inquisition) were still consulted in the hope that they could provide some of the answers, while alchemists were trying to turn base metals into gold and astrologers were studying the heavens in the belief that the conjunctions of stars and planets affected events on earth.

Nostradamus embraced the two trends of magic and academic study, confirmed in many of the beliefs that are now labelled 'superstition' but looking forward toward a new understanding of the spiritual and physical world. He may have inherited from his Jewish forbears his capacity for prediction, but his ability to hone that gift into a talent for full-blown prophecy was due, at least in part, to the intellectual stimuli of the century in which he was born.

Why has his reputation survived? And why in the twentieth century is it worth giving any credence to the convoluted verses of a man who, by his own admission, received prophetic inspiration by means of a magic ritual practised in ancient Greece over two thousand years ago? One reason may be that, although he has been sometimes mistaken and is frequently unintelligible, in the words of James Laver, one of the major commentators on the prophet and his works, 'Nostradamus could sometimes foresee the future and foresee it with an amazing particularity of detail.' He has been right in a remarkable number of cases. It is perhaps not surprising that Nostradamus scores his most direct hits with his predictions of events concerning the French monarchy and, in particular, its overthrow in the Revolution of 1789. His accounts of incidents which occurred more than two hundred years after his death are amazingly true to life.

Another reason for his continued popularity is his universality. He was not simply concerned with France, but with the rest of Europe, including Britain, and beyond. The scope of prophetic writing is generally limited to the

the dignity of man – was a significant part of this movement. And the development of the printing press subsequently made both ancient texts and modern commentaries on them widely available.

The desire for knowledge was, however, limited for the most part, to information found in books or received through divine inspiration. Experience and experiment were not considered instructive so that while people were pondering the nature of the universe, the majority of them were not doing so in anything that might be termed a scientific manner. So magic – the system of beliefs by which it is thought humans may control the natural and supernatural forces that affect their lives – was still practised. Books on the occult (many of people and location from which it springs, rather than being concerned with events on a world scale. This geographical limitation is typical of Greek, Hebrew, Celtic and American Indian prophetic traditions, among others, but the broad sweep of Nostradamus's prophetic vision makes his verses of universal interest.

And, finally, perhaps in this rational age, we are becoming aware of the reason for prophecy: to warn us of the repercussions of abandoning right living and the consequences of upsetting the balance, harmony and proper relationship between the human soul, other human beings, our environment, our planet and, ultimately, the universe.

This book is divided into two parts. The first looks at Nostradamus's life and work in the context of sixteenth-century France. The second deals with specific prophecies of past and future events. Before reviewing his life, however, it is pertinent to consider the man, as he was described by his pupil and biographer Jean Aymes de Chavigny: 'He was a man of slightly less than medium height, robust, cheerful and vigorous. His brow was high and open, his nose straight and equal, and his eyes grey and usually gentle though in anger they seemed to be flaming. He had a severe yet laughing face, so that a great humanity was obvious even while he was annoyed. His cheeks were ruddy even into old age, his beard was long and thick, his health good apart from complaints associated with age, and his senses acute. He had a good, acute mind and understood easily; his judgement was subtle, his memory excellent ... he thought a lot but spoke little .... He slept only four or five hours a night, loved and praised freedom of speech, and had a joyful hearty laugh.

'He approved of the ceremonies of the Roman church, and was a Catholic, believing that there could be no hope of salvation outside that faith. He disapproved of those who had left the bosom of the Church for the laxity and freedom of strange and damnable doctrines, affirming that they would meet an evil and pernicious end.

'I will not forget that he willingly fasted, prayed and gave alms ... when giving to the poor (toward whom he was very generous and charitable) he quoted these words from the Holy Writ: "Would you make to yourselves friends by the means of the mammon of unrighteousness?"'

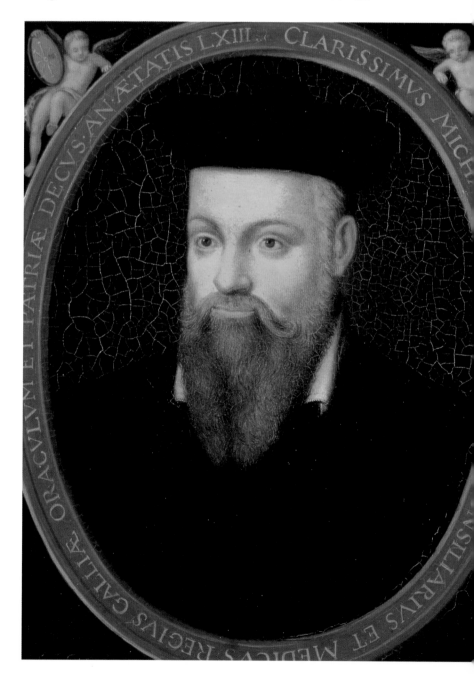

Below: An undated portrait of Nostradamus by his son César de Nostredame. His appearance with long beard, high forehead and steady gaze concurs with an early description of the prophet by his pupil Chavigny noted below left.

PART ONE

EARLY YEARS

NOSTRADAMUS WAS BORN Michel de Nostredame on 14th December 1503 in the small town of St Rémy in Provence. He was a second-generation Christian in a family of Jews. Since Biblical times the history of the Jews has been one of wandering. Deprived of secure homes in either Europe or the Middle East by adherents of both the Christian and Moslem religions, Jews spread through Europe in search of safe havens and the opportunity of earning a living. In many areas they enjoyed comparative security for a while, but the history of the Jewish people is inextricably linked with periods of oppression and persecution. They were expelled from England in 1290 and France in 1306. In 1492, the year in which the Moors were driven out of the city of Granada – their last enclave in Spain – the Spanish Jewish population of around 50,000 was given the choice: convert to Christianity or leave. In 1494 the Jews were expelled from Florence, in 1501 from Naples and in 1516 from Genoa.

Persecution of the Jews was rooted in their traditional 'differentness': their adherence to religious beliefs, which extended to dietary and culinary traditions, and their strong sense of group identity, which made them ready targets in times of national fervour. And one of their traditional occupations, that of moneylending (forbidden to Christians by canon law), aroused at best distrust and at worst open hostility. (It was, however, one of the reasons why exile tended not to be permanent: the advancement of credit and moneylending were necessary to the burgeoning business life of Europe.)

Those Jews and Moslems who chose to settle where they were and convert to Christianity were still not safe, due to the revival of the Spanish Inquisition in 1478. A medieval institution designed to combat heresy through any means its officers – papal appointees – saw fit (torture was authorized in 1252), the Inquisition had lapsed during the

Left: The exterior of the house on the Rue de Barri where Nostradamus was born and spent the early years of his life. While he was still a young boy, Nostradamus went to live with his maternal grandfather who took charge of his education until his death, at which time Nostradamus returned to this house.

Right: King Rene (1409-1480), inherited Anjou and Provence from his elder brother Louis III in 1434. Under his rule, the Jewish population were able to live without fear of persecution. (Portrait by L. Olivier.)

Below: Jews being burned alive from a wood engraving in the *Nuremburg Chronicle,* 1493. Throughout the fifteenth and sixteenth centuries, anti-Jewish feeling ran high and many Jews were tortured or killed.

fourteenth and fifteenth centuries. Its revival and the appointment as Grand Inquisitor of Tomás de Torquemada in 1483 made open profession and practice of Judaism impossible and threatened all new converts to Christianity. Those who confessed to heresy at secret trials were fined or given a variety of penances; those who failed to confess and were found guilty were burned.

One haven in the fifteenth century was Provence, under the jurisdiction of René I 'the Good', Duke of Anjou and Count of Provence and Piedmont. Although he spent the early years of his reign pressing his claims to the throne of Naples (which he lost in 1442), he devoted the latter half of his life to Provençal art and literature at his court in Aix. Not only was René himself a gifted poet, musician and

artist, but his court also attracted the cream of Europe's scholars. More importantly for the victims of persecution, René was known to be tolerant of differing religious beliefs. Here the Jews found religious freedom and the leave to practise medicine, engage in commerce and the arts, and assist in financial transactions.

On René's death in 1480, Provence passed to Charles VIII who also ascended the French throne three years later. By an edict of 1488 he decreed that all Jews must either convert to Christianity or lose all they possessed. In 1501 the edict was confirmed by Louis XII. Michel de Nostredame's two grandfathers and one of his grandmothers were among the converts. Although the date of their conversions is not known, they were registered as part of the Christian community of St Rémy by 1512.

Pierre de Nostredame was an Avignon grain dealer who moved to St Rémy with his wife Blanche (a Gentile) and son Jacques in 1495. Jacques and his wife Renée, daughter of Jean de St Rémy, were the parents of Michel de Nostredame. In accordance with Christian practice, the child was baptized (although the choice of the name Michel, after the archangel Michael, is equally acceptable to both Christian and Jewish faiths) and not circumcized. He had three brothers of whom little is known but their names – Bertrand, Hectore and Antoîne; a fourth, Jean, wrote ribald French songs and became *procureur* in the Provençal parliament.

Michel's early education was taken care of by his grandfather, Jean de St Rémy, with whom he went to live. To understand the true nature of the prophecies of Nostradamus, it is important to remember that the ancient and mystical secrets of Jewish lore – those of the Kabbalah, literally 'doctrines received from tradition' (see pages 39–40) – would have been passed on to Michel as an eldest son by his grandfather. This secret knowledge almost certainly formed the basis of the studies which

developed his later skills as a prophet. Jean de St Rémy also taught his grandson the rudiments of Latin, Greek, Hebrew, mathematics and astrology, the 'celestial science'. It was apparent that even as a child Michel had a fine intellect and a passion for star gazing. An early biographer records how, in a clear night sky, he was able to point to and name those planets whose 'conjunctions influence our life and

Above: Of great symbolic significance in Judaism is the Holy of Holies in Jerusalem where the Ark of the Covenant was enshrined. The Israelites made the ark to protect the tablets of the ten commandments during their years of wandering in the desert.

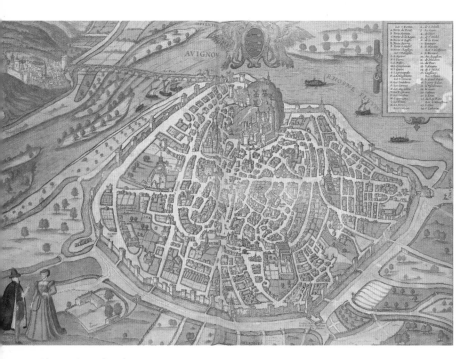

Above: A medieval map of Avignon, where Nostradamus studied for his first degree in Humanities.

Right: A pictorial representation of the universe according to Copernicus. Copernican theory, published in 1543, suggested that the stars and planets rose and set daily as a result of the rotation of the earth on its polar axis and that the apparent movement of the sun through the constellations of the zodiac could be attributed to an annual rotation of the earth around the sun.

decide our destiny'. However, Jean's sudden death forced Michel to return to his parents' home in the rue de Barri in St Rémy where his education continued under the supervision of his paternal grandfather, Pierre de Nostredame.

At the age of thirteen, Michel was ready to absorb more knowledge than was available in the town of St Rémy and he enrolled at the university of Avignon to follow a course in Humanities. In order to study the classical texts which formed the basis of the educational curriculum (the Dutch humanist and scholar Erasmus shared the views of his peers that the purpose of education was to ease contact with the past), the 'Renaissance man' had to master grammar, rhetoric, Latin, Greek, history, philosophy and poetry.

Michel passed the entrance exam in grammar, rhetoric and philosophy and began his studies. He distinguished himself quickly, reputedly sometimes taking the teacher's chair. It is also possible that he had access to the library of the papal palace which had a fine collection of occult literature. Although certain works were censored and placed on the *Index Prohibitorum*, anyone judged unlikely to be corrupted by reading forbidden titles was given

more freedom. Regardless of its source, the knowledge he expounded was almost certain to bring him to the attention of the Church authorities. According to his disciple and first biographer, Jean Aymes de Chavigny, he described to his fellow students the movements of the planets and the annual revolution of the earth round the sun, explaining that the earth was round like a ball and that the sun, when it set, illuminated the opposite hemisphere. Although the German scholar Nicholas of Cusa had suggested as early as 1440 that the earth might rotate and might not be the centre of the universe, the Polish astronomer Copernicus did not publish his findings that the sun, rather than the earth, was at the centre of the known universe, until 1543. Copernicus's delay in publishing what he proved some years before was due to his acknowledgement that his findings were at odds with Church dogma. Michel de Nostredame's family, at home in St Rémy, feared for their son's safety.

Avignon, the seat of the Popes between 1309 and 1377 and a rival papacy to that of Rome

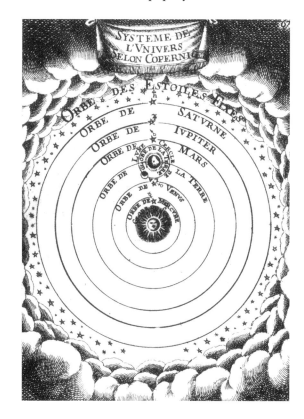

until 1417, retained a papal legate who ruled the town from the *Palais des papes* and who had his own guard of soldiers dressed in blue, red and orange livery. The power of the cardinals during the Avignon papacy was one of the reasons for the papacy's recall to Rome. A result of this supreme ecclesiastical power had been to make the town's citizens some of the most fearful and, consequently, intolerant in France. A contemporary historian drew attention to one of the scenes that contributed to its inhabitants' wariness: 'Under the central arch of the new St Michel bridge, built in 1508, hung a great cage of iron in which blasphemers were locked up before being plunged in the river Garonne to drown'.

Michel managed to evade the authorities, perhaps through his adherence to dogma and attendance at religious services, or maybe he was warned or realized that it might be wise to keep his unorthodox views to himself. As soon as he had obtained his degree in 1521, however, the family agreed that he should leave Avignon. He transferred his studies to the University of Montpellier, in preparation for his first career – that of a doctor.

Above: The Papal Palace at Avignon. As a result of troubles in Italy, Pope Clement V left Rome in 1309 and chose Avignon as a temporary seat for the pontiff. It remained so for sixty-eight years until Pope Gregory XI returned to Rome. The Palace has been described by the chronicler Froissart as the 'strongest and most beautiful house in the world.'

PLAGUE DOCTOR

WHEN NOSTRADAMUS arrived at Montpellier University to begin his medical studies in 1522, he was nineteen years old. Along with Padua and Bologna in Italy, and Paris, Montpellier had a reputation as one of the most advanced medical schools in the world. It was certainly one of the oldest: there is a tradition that a school was founded by a Talmudic scholar, a student of Rabbi Abban at Narbonne, called to the town to teach medicine there soon after 1000. Certainly the university dates from at least the twelfth century.

The medicine that Nostradamus and his colleagues were taught, however, was firmly rooted in the past and derived from Arabic translations of classical Greek texts, or vice versa, unsupplemented by knowledge gained through experience or experiment. (An early commentator, Boulenger, claimed that a reference in an ancient Greek manuscript had infinitely more weight than anything learned by experience.) Until the end of the twelfth century, medical practice was most highly developed in the east, from India through Mesopotamia and Egypt to North Africa and Spain and back along the Mediterranean coast to Constantinople. Although with the decline of the Arabic empire new centres of learning developed in the west, Arabic medical treatises were translated into Latin and – where they corroborated and furthered Greek and Roman thinking, such as in the *Canon of Medicine* by the tenth-century Persian Avicenna – absorbed into

Opposite: The Renaissance did not bring about an immediate revolution in medical theory and practice, as illustrated by Jean Corbeckon. Some advances were made in the fields of anatomy and physiology, but in a time before anaesthesia was discovered and when the transmision of infectious diseases was still unknown, no great progress could be expected. Many doctors used alchemy and magic to effect their cures.

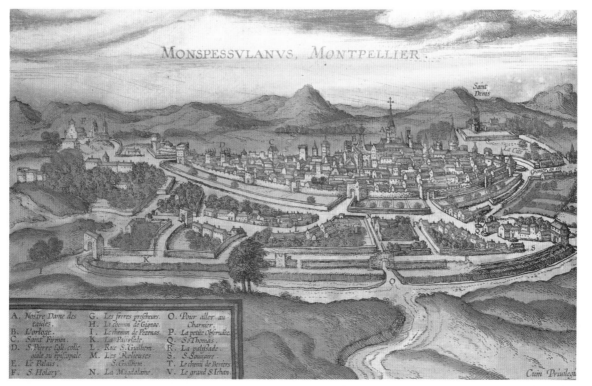

MONSPESSVLANVS, MONTPELLIER.

A. Nostre Dame des taules.
B. L'orloge.
C. Saint Firmin.
D. S. Pierre Eglise collegiale ou episcopale.
E. Le Palais.
F. S. Holary.
G. Les freres prescheurs.
H. Le chemin de Gignae.
I. Le chemin de Pezenas.
K. La Purisade.
L. Rue S. Guilhem.
M. Les Religieuses S. Guilhem.
N. La Magdalaine.
O. Pour aller au Charnier.
P. La petite Observance.
Q. S. Thomas.
R. La palisade.
S. S. Sauveure.
T. Le chemin de Besiers.
V. Le grand S. Iehan.

Cum Priuilegio

Left: Montpellier was once recommended by British physicians as a health resort for patients suffering from pulmonary complaints. This opinion has since been reversed by scientists who describe its changeable atmosphere as distinctly unhealthy!

Right: Greek doctors illustrated in an Arabian manuscript, thirteen century. Ancient Greek physicians raised medicine to the level of a science under the leadership of Hippocrates, the father of medicine. Arabian medical texts often applied and developed Greek thinking in their diagnoses and methods of treatment.

the body of medical knowledge taught in the universities.

The authority on anatomy – the identification, description and classification of the body's structures – and physiology – 'knowledge about nature' – was Aristotle. He taught anatomy through animal dissection and diagrams. Theophrastus, Aristotle's pupil, to whom he left his library, was the first master of natural history, writing classifications and descriptions of more than 500 plants and producing what was almost certainly the first herbal. The authorities on 'pure' medicine were Hippocrates and Galen. Hippocrates, whose works date from the fifth and fourth centuries BC, was first and foremost concerned with diagnosis, which was reached through observation and description, and with treatment. His analyses and descriptions of some diseases are recognizable even today. He also posited that the

Right: A series of three pictures taken from the *Canon of Medicine* by Avicenna to illustrate the treatment for a fracture-dislocation of the spinal column. Avicenna is generally regarded as the greatest of the Moslem philosophers and physicians. The *Canon*, his most famous work, was still in use as a medical text book in some universities in France in the seventeenth century.

body was governed by four humours – blood, phlegm, and black and yellow bile. Galen, whose teachings held sway for some 1,400 years, is probably the most influential figure in medicine. From his studies of monkeys and dogs, he demonstrated the importance of the spinal cord in muscle activity, described the functioning of the kidneys and bladder and correctly identified that the arteries carried blood, not air.

This, then, was the intellectual milieu of the 1520s in which Nostradamus found himself. Great steps forward in medicine were around the corner: the Flemish anatomist Vesalius published his *Structure of the Human Body*, a series of accurate anatomical drawings made following dissections of humans in 1543, paving the way for a reappraisal of Galen. And the Swiss-born Paracelsus, who died in 1541 and publicly burned the works of Avicenna and Galen, stressed the importance of treating disease with chemical compounds and identified mineral deficiencies as the cause of some ailments. For the period of his medical education, however, Nostradamus's professors taught a mixture of alchemy, astrology, primitive surgery (in contrast to most universities, dissection *was* carried out at Montpellier) and the 'set texts'. Minor ailments were usually dealt with by herbalists or apothecaries; childbirth was supervised by the midwives; the treatment of anything more serious, however, was somewhat hit and miss.

To enrol in the medical faculty Nostradamus first had to find a *procureur* – a student elected for administrative duties – to appear with him before the chancellor to establish his credentials: his date of birth, his legitimacy, his professed Roman Catholicism, an arts degree and his ignorance of any kind of manual work. If this last condition could not be fulfilled he must have studied philosophy for at least two years. When these formalities were completed, Nostradamus appeared before the board of the medical faculty to be questioned by one of the professors on rhetoric and philosophy from the works of Cicero and Aristotle. After giving satisfactory answers he was allowed to write his name on the register of the faculty and accepted as capable of following the three-year course. Nostradamus absorbed knowledge easily and if he had any difficulty, it was in the unquestioning acceptance of the ancient authorities. His intellectual insights almost certainly directed his own mind toward the creation of medical techniques which only later were absorbed into an accepted body of medical doctrine.

The degree examinations themselves were conducted by dispute. From eight a.m. until midday Nostradamus answered the professors' questions, convincing them of the extent and depth of his learning. He may not have agreed with their prescribed authorities, but his scholarship and dedication were indisputable. At the degree ceremony the chancellor awarded Nostradamus the red-hooded robe of the scholar, after which he received the congratulations of his fellow students.

Although Nostradamus now had a degree in medicine, his almost exclusively theoretical knowledge did not entitle him to use a scalpel or carry out an operation without the assistance of a barber or barber–surgeon. If medical practice was somewhat backward, then, in the absence of antiseptics, with no recognition of the importance of sterility and a restricted knowledge in many cases of how the body worked, surgery was still in the dark ages. Bologna was the only university in which surgery was taught as a discipline; elsewhere it was deemed a craft, best learned through serving an apprenticeship. In some parts of Europe, the surgeons had formed themselves into a 'higher division' of the barber–surgeon guilds but often the two were indistinguishable. Barbers were allowed to shave, cut and bleed patients, in addition to pulling teeth.

For three months Nostradamus had to teach, under supervision, in the medical school after which he could sit four examinations *per intentionem* (essentially an interrogation by four professors on four different illnesses). A week later, he went through the ordeal for a fifth illness, 'pricked' with a pin from a medical treatise, for which he had to prescribe a remedy. That over, Nostradamus was given a quotation

Left: An illuminated manuscript of Anatomical Man shows how the planets and their aspects were thought to exert an influence over the internal workings of the body (undated).

by Hippocrates on which he had to prepare a thesis for the following day when, in the chapel of St Michel in the church of Notre-Dame-des-Tables, from midday until four p.m. he underwent a further 'dispute' with his professors. The first part of his studies now over, Nostradamus received his licence to practise medicine from the archbishop of Montpellier. What he now needed was practical experience, for which he did not have long to wait.

Plague had first reached Europe from Constantinople in the 1340s. The Black Death of 1347–50 affected every area of the European mainland and Great Britain and may have reduced the European population by as much as one-third. Although there were periods of respites, it is likely that the plague did not really die out. Certainly there were outbreaks of varying degrees of virulence until the eighteenth century. Today, plague is limited to the tropics and occurs only in areas where sanitary conditions are poor, but in the thirteenth to nineteenth centuries that was the case in most of the towns of Europe, particularly in summer. Since the cause of the disease was not known –

it was only discovered in the nineteenth century that bubonic plague is transmitted to people through fleas which feed on infected rats – treatment was almost always ineffective. In an era when medical practice was still rooted in the belief that disease was either a punishment from God, or the result of an imbalance in the body's four humours, bleeding (or a purgative or emetic) was one of the preferred remedies. (This notion was one derived from Hippocrates and apparently unquestioned; Hippocrates prescribed black hellebore as a purgative, white as an emetic.) This simply had the effect of weakening those stricken with the disease still further.

Plague hit southern France in the 1520s. Scarcely had Nostradamus received his licence than *le charbon*, named for the black abcesses which appeared in the palm of the hand, armpit or groin and were the first signs of infection, reached Montpellier. A contemporary account of a death by plague describes the corpse as half the colour of the sky and half full of violet blood.

In contrast to most other doctors who

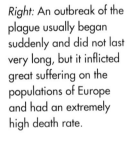

Right: An outbreak of the plague usually began suddenly and did not last very long, but it inflicted great suffering on the populations of Europe and had an extremely high death rate.

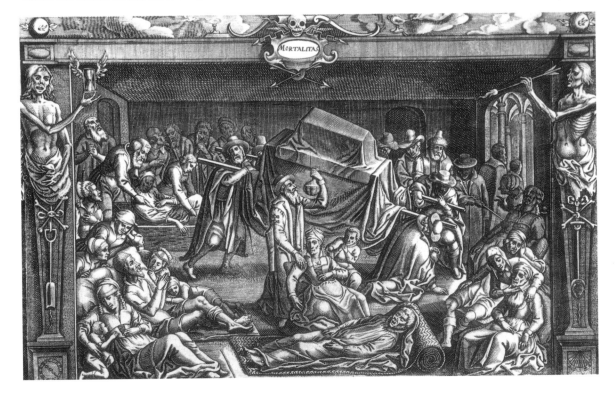

*Habit des Medecins, et autres personnes,
qui visitent les Pestiferes, Il est de
marroqûin de leuant, le masque a les yeux
de cristal, et un long nez rempli de parfuins*

attempted to treat the plague, Nostradamus chose not to wear the traditional garb of a multicoloured shirt soaked in supposedly magical juices and stained with different coloured powders, over which was worn a tunic of red leather, believed to be impervious to tainted air. With bells or cymbals attached to his shoes to herald his arrival, a sponge tied around his nose to keep out evil humours and chewing a clove of garlic against infection, the plague doctor moved through the streets dispensing advice. He was more often than not welcomed with a hail of abuse and a variety of projectiles.

Nostradamus's methods, too, were unconventional. He bled no-one; more importantly, he recognized the importance of hygiene. In his travels through the countryside as he followed the progress of the disease, perhaps he noticed, or perhaps his developing precognitive skills told him, that those people who lived isolated lives in the countryside, away from overcrowding in the towns where human, animal and vegetable waste were concentrated, fared better. He appears to have prescribed clean water and fresh air and stressed the importance of a healthy diet. (Hippocrates had also advocated clean air and a healthy diet as essential to well-being, but Nostradamus may have been the first to stress them in the treatment of plague victims.) Nostradamus gave orders that straw mattresses, and, in some cases, the entire contents of a house, should be burned. He also proposed the isolation of infected cases.

The concept of isolation was not new. Lepers had been isolated for centuries and so successful had the practice been that leprosy had all but died out in Europe by 1500. Isolation had also been tried during the Black Death. Now, along with a host of other measures, it was revived on a more or less systematic basis, depending on the authority of the town or city. In some areas guards were posted at the town gates, or some miles outside them, to stop anyone showing signs of, or even suspected of carrying, the disease from entering.

Left: The Plague doctor. This particular outfit was worn by the doctors of Lyon when they visited their patients. The suit was made of fine leather, with crystal eyes set into the headdress and a long nose which held perfumes to purify the contaminated air.

Below: A medieval map of Marseilles, France's oldest city and seaport. The isolation hospital, established for those suffering from the bubonic plague, can be seen on the left of the hilly peninsula in the foreground. An epidemic of the plague in a seaport was especially dangerous because rats spread the disease by ship from port to port.

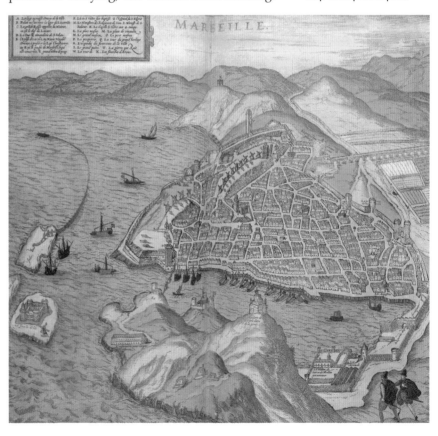

Right: Popular superstition held that disease was a scourge of God. This symbolic illustration shows the wrath of God in the form of a flying demon with a serpent's tail striking a sinful human with disease.

Far right: The Provencal Rose. Although the rose possesses no known medicinal or curative powers, large quantities of rose petals were the main ingredients of the rose-pills prescribed and made by Nostradamus as a preventive or cure during outbreaks of the plague.

Right: Detail of a man picking a rose from a Normandy manuscript dating from the late fifteenth century. One of the most beautiful of all flowers, the rose is a symbol of fragrance and loveliness.

Citizens were offered money to burn soiled clothes and linen, and to clean houses and perfume them with herbs and scented potions. Brothels were closed. The infected were instructed to carry red, white or black sticks and to put crosses on their doors.

There were several reasons why these approaches often failed to work. Firstly, in the atmosphere of panic that accompanied the first appearance of the plague, they were often ignored. Secondly, many people, including some of the doctors, believed that the successful treatment of infection was due to the cure being administered at the right time, astrologi-cally. And, finally, when most people thought that plague was the manifestation of the wrath of God, what good was treatment? The fact that Nostradamus insisted on strict adherence to these preventive measures laid the foundations of his success as a plague doctor wherever he travelled through Provence.

Nostradamus was reputed to carry his own plague powder which may have been some form of disinfectant. He also carried and dispensed 'rose pills' which were to be kept under the tongue, but not swallowed, at all times. Whether these were successful in their own right – the mixture does contain high concentrations of vitamin C, which may have helped those who were already strong enough to fend off the disease – or simply as part of his total treatment regime is uncertain.

Formula of rose pills:

1 oz sawdust from green cypress

6 oz iris of Florence

3 oz cloves, powdered

3 drams odorated calamus

6 drams lign-aloes

300–400 roses plucked before dawn, pulverized and kept from exposure to air

The ingredients should be mixed together and formed into pills or lozenges. Nostradamus pointed out that they could be made only once a year, when (Provence) roses were in bloom.

Nostradamus left Montpellier when the worst of the plague was over and followed the course of the sickness to the small hamlets and towns on the river Garonne and its tributaries. He lived for a time in the rue Triperie, Carcassone, where he is reported as prescribing a cure for the bishop, Monseigneur Armanien de Fays. The nature of the bishop's malady is not clear, although the 'cure' consisted of a pomade made from lapis lazuli, coral and leaf gold – a 'veritable elixir of life' – which was reputed to 'rejuvenate the sad, make joyful the melancholy, render the timid audacious, the taciturn affable and the surly sweet and kindly ... retard old age and a grey beard and augment the sperm'.

As Nostradamus travelled throughout plague-ridden France during his first years as a doctor, he charged only those who could afford it for medical treatment, but often received, in addition to his fees, substantial gifts in appreciation of his skills. Many of these gifts he distributed among the poor and needy. He spent some time in Narbonne, where there was a large Jewish population and where schools of Talmudists and alchemists flourished, then visited Bordeaux before arriving back in Avignon. He almost certainly consulted with many of the specialist apothecaries in every town, perhaps learning new 'recipes' for treatments and sharing some of his own.

He also kept on the right side of the ecclesiastical authorities. The Protestant reformation was spreading. A Catholic whose family had so recently been converted from Judaism, and someone whose talents could easily arouse jealousy and mistrust, Nostradamus made it clear that he was on the side of the Church in any religious dispute. An efficacious remedy, pomade or potion must have made many a bishop or prelate kindly disposed toward him.

After about four years the plague seemed to have run its course and Nostradamus returned

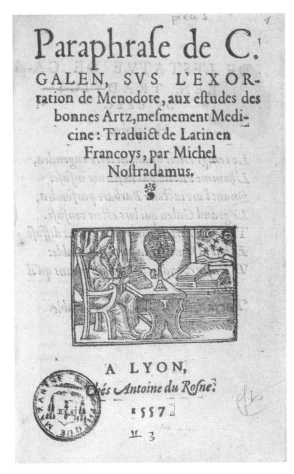

Left: The title page of Nostradamus's Latin translation of a medical work by the Greek doctor, Galen. At the time Nostradamus was studying, Galen's works were essential academic texts.

to Montpellier, with a wealth of experience and accumulated knowledge, to take his master's degree. On 23rd October 1529 he once again inscribed his name on the university register. His highly unorthodox methods and the success they had brought him as a plague doctor had not endeared him to his professors, but they could hardly exclude someone of such obvious learning. He was led by a procession of the entire faculty to the church of St Firmin, where he was again subjected to a rigorous oral examination at the end of which he was given the square hat, ring, girdle and a volume of the works of Hippocrates, signifying his status as a doctor of medicine.

In the following year Nostradamus taught in the faculty of medicine as a professor, but in 1531, unable to tolerate the intellectual restrictions, he saddled his mule, packed a small bag of books and scientific instruments and left Montpellier for the last time.

Above: Hans Holbein's portrait of Erasmus, the foremost Christian humanist of the Renaissance. Erasmus looked to Greek and Latin authors for inspiration in an effort to restore early Christian ideals and wrote new studies of the Old and New Testaments.

stayed there. He was an outstanding exponent of the physics and metaphysics of Aristotle (and the first person to bring Aristotle's theories on tragedy to a French audience) and well known for his commentaries on many classical texts. He entered into lively intellectual debate with the Dutch humanist and thinker Erasmus, defending those writers who borrowed the stylistic excesses of Cicero for their own work, which had earned them the condemnation of Erasmus. So Nostradamus went to Agen, found lodgings and often visited Scaliger, his wife Adriete de Loubejac and their two sons. (Scaliger's son Joseph also became an outstanding classical scholar.)

Nostradamus was thirty. He had devoted good years of his life to healing the sick; he had learned much from his travels; and it was time to cease wandering. The importance of family life in Jewish culture may also have encouraged him to look for a wife at this time. He married a young woman of good family who bore him a son and a daughter. He established a medical practice, enjoyed family life and thrived on the intellectual companionship of his friend Scaliger. Then plague came to Agen. He resumed his former speciality, treating many of the plague's victims, but could not save those closest to him. His wife and children died in

For two years he wandered through Languedoc and Provence, visiting La Rochelle, Bordeaux and Toulouse and treating many important people in their castles and country houses. While in Toulouse he received an invitation from Julius Caesar Scaliger, a renowned humanist scholar who lived in Agen and had heard of Nostradamus's reputation, to visit his home. An Italian, Scaliger had gone to Agen in the service of the Bishop, liked the town and

quick succession. Bereft and grieving, stricken with remorse and guilt for their deaths, he was then sued by his wife's family for the return of her dowry. To add to his misfortunes, the Inquisition wanted to question him about a casual criticism he had made about a statue of the Virgin Mary – a comment made three years before which had referred to a sculptor's poor workmanship and which the sculptor had apparently been waiting his time to avenge. The final straw was a quarrel with the irascible Scaliger who, sooner or later it seemed, quarrelled with everyone. Nostradamus saddled his mule, packed his books and left Agen. This time he travelled for eight years through France to Italy and Sicily, meeting apothecaries and physicians who were able to increase his already extensive medical knowledge.

In 1544 Nostradamus was summoned to a new outbreak of plague in Marseilles. In November of that year there had been devastating floods in southern France. The river Rhône was a raging torrent and much of the countryside was under water. The rising water had breached the walls of Avignon. St Rémy was accessible only by boat and the floating corpses of men, women and animals meant an inevitable spread of disease. Marseilles was, in normal circumstances, an agreeable place, a seaport where he found interesting ingredients for medicines and a plethora of apothecaries' shops. The town had a substantial Jewish population and scholars in medicine and astrology. Nostradamus considered settling there, but a deputation arrived from Aix-en-Provence asking for his help. Many of the town's inhabitants had died or fled; there was no longer a parliament or any court of justice and the town gates had been closed for 200 days. Contemporary accounts report that, with a hopeless sense of modesty, women of the town were to be seen sewing themselves into their shrouds. In the company of an apothecary,

Left: Herbalist and Apothecary from "le Proprietaire des Choses", published in 1500, in Paris. Most of the medicines during the Middle Ages were made by herbalists and apothcaries using recipes that had been passed down for generations. Certain innovative doctors, among them Nostradamus and Paracelsus, devised and prepared their own remedies, often with great success.

Joseph Turel Mercurin, Nostradamus set out for Aix. His treatments were so successful that the town's grateful citizens awarded him a life pension. But he chose not to stay there.

Nostradamus reached Salon, a town to the north of Marseilles, then was summoned to Lyons to cope with an epidemic. Controversy awaited him. Another doctor, Antoîne Sarrazin, whose medical practices were very different from his own, disputed with Nostradamus the most effective way to treat plague victims, forcing the town's authorities to choose between them. Nostradamus's reputation secured him the task and his own medical remedies had their usual successful results. The resentful Sarrazin accused Nostradamus of practising magic, a charge which he successfully rebutted but which made him uneasy. Laden with gifts from the people of Lyons and, thanks to the people of Aix financially secure, he decided to abandon his first great career. He returned to Salon, which was to be his home until his death.

Opposite page: Julius Caesar Scaliger (1484-1558) was a classical scholar of Italian descent whose studies included botany, zoology, grammar and literary criticism. He left Italy in 1525 to become a French citizen and settled in Agen where he took up a position as the Bishop's physician.

PROPHET AND PSYCHIC

At the age of forty-four Nostradamus abandoned his life as a wandering plague doctor and settled in the Provençal town of Salon to concentrate on the writings that have brought him lasting fame. He married a young widow of the town, Anne Ponsart Gemelle, and when they set up home Nostradamus converted an upstairs room into a study filled with books and all kinds of astrological and occult instruments. From this room he could observe the stars and planets and thus was able to calculate the most auspicious times to perform the rituals which brought him prophetic inspiration.

The origins of Nostradamus's prophetic gifts are uncertain. He may have inherited them from his ancestors; he may have had access to works which have now been lost, but which somehow showed him the way. He clearly felt that his gift was a mixture of inherited power, education and training. In his epistle to Henri II of 1557, he wrote: 'It is very true Sir, that by my natural instinct given me by my progenitors, I did think I could foretell anything; but having made an agreement between this said instinct of mine, and a long calculation of art, and by a great tranquillity and repose of mind, by emptying my soul of all care, I have foretold most part of these *ex tripode oeneo* [by the brass tripod, see page 32].' What is certain, however, is that he had some gift of premonition – demonstrated long before he started work on the prophecies which made his second (and enduring) reputation – a gift or talent which R. J. Stewart, the author of the seminal work on the subject *Prophecy* calls an 'inherent inner ability' or 'genetic inheritance'.

The line between psychic and prophet is fine and often blurred only by the subject matter and timing of the precognition. Psychic powers reveal events of an immediate and often isolated nature while prophetic skills delve deep into the future on a more global scale. Tales abound of what might be termed Nostradamus's

SIXTVS · V · PONT · OPT · MAX

Opposite page: 'Spirits in Water'. Dario Poli's individual interpretation of Nostradamus's vision as he gazes into the brass bowl of water and sees, as through a cloud, spirits of the future from whom he receives prophecy, conjured in part, by the practice of ancient ritual magic.

Left: Sixtus V was unanimously elected as successor to Pope Gregory XIII in 1585. As Pope, his strong measures in dealing with lawlessness following the Counter Reformation eventually restored peace and safety to the papal states.

Right: Detail of a man and a pig from a fifteenth century illuminated manuscript.

psychic rather than prophetic skills. One day while travelling through Italy, he saw a group of monks walking toward him. As they approached he dropped to his knees before one young man, to the surprised laughter of his friends for the young monk was a former pig-keeper named Felice Peretti. When asked to explain his action, Nostradamus replied that he knelt before 'His Holiness'. In 1585, Felice Peretti was elected pope, taking the name Sixtus V.

On one of his visits to Catherine de Medici's court, as he was sitting one evening in his lodgings, Nostradamus heard a loud commotion outside. It was a frightened servant who had lost his master's dog. Nostradamus opened the window and directed him to the road to Orleans where he would find the dog, still on its leash. The story, and Nostradamus's reputation, spread rapidly.

Sometimes his sixth sense operated in a more humorous vein. When he was sitting outside his house in Salon one cool evening, a pretty young girl passed by on her way to the forest to collect firewood. She smiled sweetly, 'Bonsoir, Monsieur de Nostredame'; 'Bonsoir, fillette' Nostradamus replied. Some time later the young girl returned, looking flushed and carrying a bundle of firewood, 'Bonsoir, Monsieur de Nostredame' she greeted him. 'Bonsoir, petite femme' Nostradamus replied dryly.

As his reputation as a clairvoyant spread, so too did the number of people who felt they must try to catch him out. A certain Seigneur de Florinville who lived in Fains Castle in Lorraine was confident he could expose the doctor's psychic inadequacy and invited him to supper during his travels in the region. On their way through the farmyard he asked Nostradamus whether they would be served the black pig or the white pig at table that night. Nostradamus replied that it would be

the black pig, since the white pig would be eaten by a wolf. De Florinville immediately instructed his cook to kill and cook the white pig. As they sat down to eat de Florinville commented, with a sly grin, that the white pig had survived being caught by a wolf for they were about to eat it. Nostradamus insisted that the black pig was on the table. De Florinville called his cook who revealed that the white pig had indeed been killed for the table, but that a young pet wolf, belonging to a servant in the household, had taken it from the spit. He had, therefore, been forced to kill the black pig which they were about to eat.

Once he had settled in Salon innkeepers marvelled at the number of travellers who came to the town singing his praises. Nostradamus, who only wanted to read and study, was unable to leave the house without being surrounded by a crowd asking questions: Would the jam set? Would a sick infant die of colic? As well as simple requests for his psychic insights there were increasing demands for demonstrations of his astrological powers. Parents besieged him to cast horoscopes for their children. Unhappy lovers knocked at his door asking whether the stars might favour reconciliation. Farmers wanted to know if the weather would be fair, and if their olive trees would be fruitful. Gardeners did not plant cabbages, girls take fiancés nor boys choose a job without consulting Nostradamus. There were no limits to their requests and no limits to the callers who arrived looking for 'le prophète' at the tall house in the narrow street off the place de la Poissonerie.

Nostradamus published his first work, an almanac, in 1550. It contained twelve quatrains (four-line verses), one for each month of the year, and was a series of astrological predictions about local matters – weather, agriculture, business, finance and health tips – for the coming year. It was an immediate success, so much so that he produced an almanac every year until his death. Nostradamus's almanacs were not unique: the almanac was probably the most common form of printed material in circulation in the sixteenth century. Most dealt with similar subjects: the weather, times for planting, prominent local marriages and deaths; the majority were written by charlatans but, to their avid consumers, they were an essential purchase. (It was estimated that at the end of the sixteenth century, one in three households in Britain possessed or had access to an almanac.) The success of the quatrain formula led Nostradamus to retain it in his major work, the *Centuries.*

In addition to the almanacs, from 1554 Nostradamus published a series of more ambitious, but less successful, *Présages* (prognostications). In spite of the numbers produced (these were the sixteenth-century blockbusters), few

of these publications survive, presumably because the ephemeral nature of their contents led people to believe they had no real value once they were out of date. Also in 1554, or thereabouts, a young man called Jean Aymes de Chavigny gave up his position as mayor in the city of Beaune and came to study astrology and astronomy as a disciple of Nostradamus. He helped Nostradamus prepare his best-known work for publication.

In 1555 Mace Bonhomme, a Lyons printer, published the *Centuries.* The title derives from the inclusion of one hundred quatrains in each volume. The 1555 edition of the *Centuries* contained only three 'centuries' and part of a fourth, but by the time the final edition was published in 1557 Nostradamus had completed more than ten 'centuries' containing nearly one thousand predictions. Nostradamus described how he arrived at his predictions in the first two quatrains of the work.

Above: It is not known exactly how many editions of the *Centuries* exist, but this particular edition was published in 1566. The sensation the book created in France when it was first released quickly spread to the rest of Europe. The text was used as a French primer in schools throughout France until the eighteenth century.

Left: An illustration taken from a nineteenth century edition of the *Centuries*, showing Nostradamus receiving a prophesy from a sybil who holds a laurel branch in the manner of the Greek oracle at Delphi.

Estant assis de nuict secret estude
Seul reposé sur la selle d'aerain;
Flambe exiguë sortant de solitude
Fait prosperer qui n'est à croire vain.
CI Q1

Seated at night in my secret study
Alone, reposing over the brass tripod,
A slender flame leaps out of the solitude
Making me pronounce what should not be
believed in vain.

The divining rod in the hand is placed in the
middle of the tripod's legs
I moisten the hem of my robe and foot with
water
Great fear makes my hand tremble:
Divine splendour. God sits nearby.

What was the nature of the prophetic experience in the attic room? According to Nostradamus he was in an inspired mental state, as if in a trance. Perhaps he used incantations to focus his mind; whatever his methods, as the visions came to him he wrote them down, probably in note form, and incorporated them later into his various works on prophecy.

In the Preface to the first edition Nostradamus revealed that he had kept the contents of the *Centuries* secret for many years because he feared that 'those of the present Reign, Sect, Religion and Faith, would find it so disagreeing with their fancies, that they would condemn that which future ages shall find and know to be true.' He had decided to publish, however, because 'the future events, chiefly the

Above: In his attic, Nostradamus made careful preparations before relaxing his mind and slipping into a prophetic trance.

Right: Prophecy was not unique to Nostradamus. In this illustration – an allegorical representation of prophecy from a sixteenth century Persian manuscript – a ruler with a sickle and a rose (emblems of peace and prosperity) stands on the bodies of slain men.

Alone at night in his study, surrounded by his books and instruments, Nostradamus gazes into a bowl of water standing on a brass tripod. As he fixes his concentration the water becomes cloudy and he is able to see, 'the great and sad events, the prodigious and calamitous accidents' that will befall future generations.

La verge en main mise au milieu des
BRANCHES
De l'onde il moulle & le limbe & le pied:
Un peur & voix fremissant par les
manches:
Splendeur divine. Le devin pres s'assied.
CI Q2

most urgent and those which I foresaw (whatever human mutations happened) would not offend the hearers ...'

The scope of the *Centuries* was vast: Nostradamus extended his prophetic horizons to embrace not only France but the rest of Europe and parts of Africa and Asia; modern interpretations suggest that many of the quatrains also refer to the Americas. Not only were they geographically broad in scale, but they also dealt with events from the contemporary to those in a distant future (see pages 138–41). To protect himself from charges of heresy by the Inquisition, and also perhaps to indulge his learning, Nostradamus wrote the *Centuries* in a mixture of French, Greek, Latin and Italian. He used anagrams, initials and odd literary devices within a grammatical structure that conformed to no rules. In addition, his visions of the future sometimes embraced objects and concepts of which he had no first-hand knowledge – flight, for example (see page 101), or the

atomic bomb (see page 99). He was, literally, groping for words. The result was an obscure jumble of verses which were largely incoherent.

Despite his precautions and reservations, the *Centuries* were a huge success. His biographer Chavigny said of this period: 'He kept them [the prophecies] a long time ... thinking that the novelty of the matter would not fail to arouse infinite detractions, calumnies and attacks .... In the end vanquished by the desire he had to be useful to the public, he published them; and immediately their noise and renown ran through the mouths of our compatriots and of strangers with the greatest wonder.'

By 1556 the *Centuries* had attracted interest all over France and were all the rage at the French court. The Queen, Catherine de Medici, sent for Nostradamus. She had horses posted for him to halve the travel time from Provence to Paris to a month. Catherine was concerned with two pressing matters: Nostradamus's prediction that her husband, the king, would die in

Above: This engraving by Hogenberg depicts the tournament of the 30th July 1559, in which Henri II of France was mortally wounded by a splinter from the lance of his opponent, Count Montgomery. Henri's unfortunate death was predicted by Nostradamus and fulfilled within the prophet's lifetime.

combat and the destinies of their seven Valois children. She had every reason to be worried. Luc Gauric, an Italian astrologer, had also told Catherine that Henri would be involved in a dangerous confrontation shortly after he became king. He even provided a horoscope in Latin which specifically warned Henri to avoid any combat in an enclosed space around his forty-first year, suggesting that at such a time he would be susceptible to a head wound which could cause blindness or death. Catherine felt that it was imperative to question Nostradamus as soon as possible.

Le lion jeune le vieux surmontera,
En champ bellique par singulier duelle:
Dans caige d'or les yeux lui crevera,
Deux classes une, puis mourir, morte cruelle.
CI Q35

The young lion will overcome the older one,
In a field of combat by a single duel,
In a golden cage he will pierce his eye
Two wounds in one, then he will die a cruel
    death.

At the meeting between Henri and Nostradamus, the King expressed little interest in the prediction of his own death, remarking that he would prefer death in combat to a 'natural' death, as long as he kept his honour and his opponent was brave and valiant. The audience was brief and Henri gave Nostradamus one hundred gold crowns for his pains. Catherine, no doubt, had more questions to ask Nostradamus but he must have been able, at least for a time, to allay the Queen's fears and satisfy her questions concerning the fate of her children.

His visit was short. Warned that his activities had come to the attention of the Paris justices and in any case anxious to get to work on the forthcoming second edition of the *Centuries*,

Right: Members of King Henri II's Scottish Guard, who formed part of his personal bodyguard and of which Count Montgomery was a captain.

Nostradamus returned to Salon. This second, enlarged edition was prefaced by an epistle to King Henri who died before the book was printed. What is remarkable about the epistle is that Nostradamus appears to refer to the French Revolution in amazing detail.

In 1559 the French court moved to St Germain-en-Laye for the summer where a double wedding celebration was to take place. The King's daughter, Marguerite, was to marry the Duke of Savoy and his sister, Elizabeth, was to be wed (by proxy) to Philip of Spain who

declined to travel to Paris to meet his bride. As part of the celebrations, a jousting tournament had been set up in the rue St Antoine near the Palais des Tournelles. In the late afternoon of the second day Henri, an excellent jouster, was in combat with the Earl of Montgomery, captain of his Scottish Guard and a keen sportsman. Henri wore a golden helmet above his armour and bore a lion rampant on his shield. Montgomery, several years his junior, also displayed a lion on his shield. The light was fading and the result was a draw.

Henri wanted to settle the contest with another bout. Montgomery, probably aware of the prediction, was not so keen. Henri insisted. They entered the lists once more and as the two men on their horses thundered past each other

TOVRNELLES

on their third encounter, their lances made contact. Montgomery's lance snapped and splintered. One of the splinters entered Henri's visor and pierced his eye and brain; another lodged itself in his throat. In agonizing pain Henri fell from his horse into the arms of his grooms. 'The young lion' had indeed overcome 'the older one'. Henri died 'a cruel death' ten days later from 'two wounds in one.' Every detail of Nostradamus's prophesy had been fulfilled. That night an effigy of the prophet was burned in the streets of Paris by angry crowds who called for his investigation before the Inquisition.

Catherine's support almost certainly saved Nostradamus; the Queen turned her wrath on Montgomery, who fled France for England. Honourable in defeat, Henri had ordered that no harm should come to Montgomery; Catherine, however, wanted her revenge. Fifteen years later, when the Huguenots of

Normandy revolted, Montgomery returned to France. In May 1574 Montgomery and his supporters were in the fortress of Domfront close to two cities they had taken. Surrounded by royal troops and unable to withstand a siege or find a means of escape, Montgomery was forced to yield the fortress. As part of the terms of the surrender Montgomery's life was to be spared, but Catherine, hearing of his presence in France, ordered his arrest. On 27th May 1574, Montgomery was seized in his bed by six noblemen of the royal army.

Above: The Death of Henri II. After the accident, Henri languished in agony for ten days and died on the 10th July 1559, at the age of forty. The splinter from Montgomery's lance had lodged in his brain and was impossible to remove.

Below: In the Wars of Religion (1562-1598), French Catholics and Huguenots fought each other in a series of violent encounters. The Catholics organized the Holy League while the Protestants had a succession of leaders including Henri of Navarre. His victory over the Holy League, followed by his accession to the throne, ended the thirty-six-year struggle for power.

Below: Mary Queen of Scots with Francis II of France. Mary was sixteen and Francis just fourteen when they were married.

Celui qu'en luitte & fer au faict bellique
Aura porté plus grand que luile prix;
De nuict au lict six lui feront la pique,
Nud sans harnois subit sera surprins.
CIII Q30

He who in a struggle on martial field,
Shall have carried off the prize from one greater
than he,
Shall be taken by six men by night,
Suddenly, naked and without armour.

The Earl of Montgomery was beheaded on Catherine's orders.

The accuracy of the prediction regarding Henri's death and his popularity with Catherine sealed Nostradamus's position as court astrologer. The *Centuries* themselves also seemed to shed some light on at least one of the Queen's children:

Premier fils veufve malheureux marriage
Sans nuls enfans deux isles en discorde,
Avant dixhuict incompetant eage,
De l'autre pres plus bas sera l'accord.
CX Q 39

The first son, a widow, an unhappy marriage
without any children: two islands in discord.
Before eighteen years of age while still a minor:
Of the other even lower will be the [marriage]
agreement.

The quatrain refers to Francis II, the sickly eldest son of Henri and Catherine de Medici who succeeded to the French throne on his father's death. Born in 1544, Francis was married to Mary Queen of Scots, two years his senior, in 1558. (Mary, the daughter of the Frenchwoman Mary of Guise, in spite of succeeding to the Scottish throne shortly after her birth, had been brought up at the French court.) Although the widowed Catherine acted as Regent and Francis was in any case under the control of his uncles (also members of the Guise family), there was much concern at Court about Francis's poor health, which fitted him neither for kingship nor for the marriage which had politically united France and Scotland but which had brought no heirs. In the speculative atmosphere brought about by Henri's untimely death and the manner in which it had been predicted, quatrain 39 started to take on a new significance. The anxious courtiers did not have long to wait. Francis died less than two years after becoming king, and – as predicted – before his eighteenth birthday.

Mary returned to Scotland confident of Catholic support in France and with a claim to the English throne through her father, James V of Scotland, grandson of Henry VII. Mary posed a threat to Elizabeth I and her Protestant kingdom that she was to pay for with years of

imprisonment and eventually her life. Francis's ten-year-old brother, who succeeded to the throne as Charles IX, was betrothed to Elizabeth of Austria at the even younger (lower) age of eleven.

By no means have all the prophecies of Nostradamus been so clearly understood or so accurately fulfilled. A sufficient number have, however, satisfied the research of generations of scholars and the general public to ensure that the 'seer of Salon' holds a special place in the study of prophets and their works. Many of his predictions are still, as the discussions in part two indicate, matters of lively debate.

Left: After the short reign of Francis II, Catherine's second son, Charles, became king of France. Charles IX is remembered for authorising the massacre of the Protestants on the Eve of St Bartholomew on the advice of his mother.

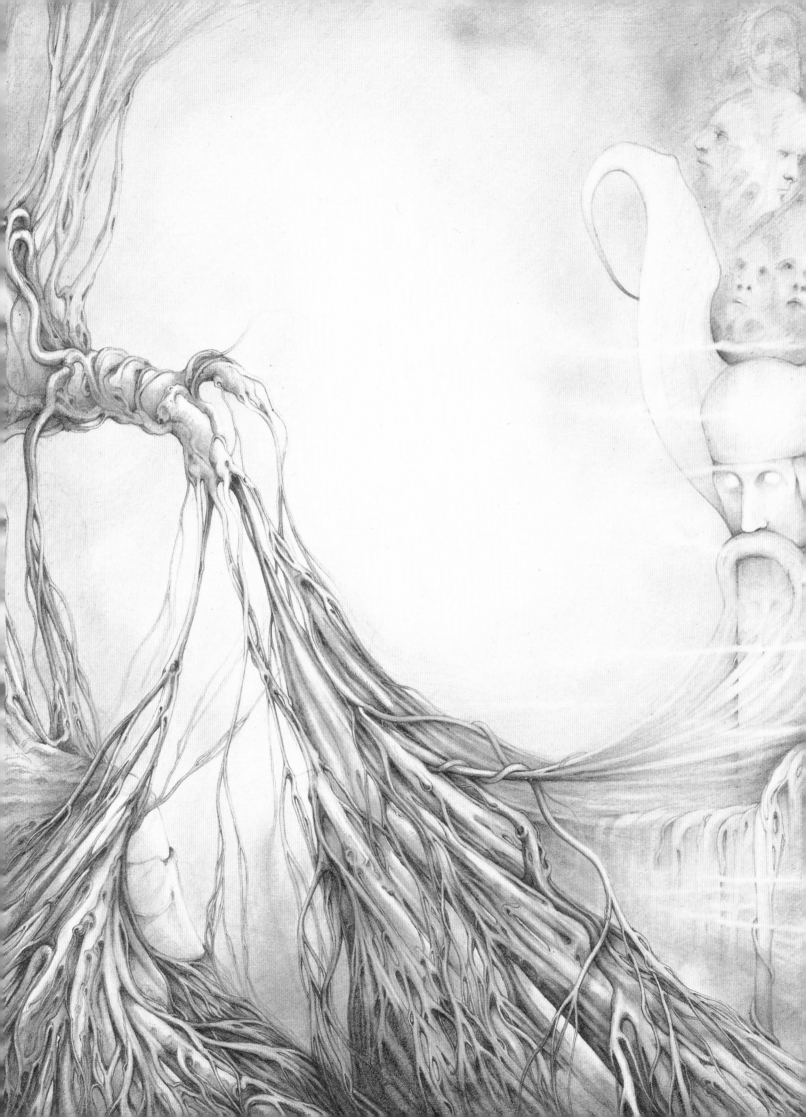

OCCULTIST AND MAGICIAN

WAS NOSTRADAMUS a magician? He was born at a time when the Renaissance spirit of enquiry was already challenging the rigid and unquestioning intellectual attitudes of the Middle Ages. The knowledge that came with new discoveries, such as that of America, raised the hope that the study of all arts and sciences might eventually lead to a perfect understanding of the natural world and an appreciation of man's nobility and capacities in a coherent and unified system.

As a Jew by family and heredity, Nostradamus was acquainted with the traditions of his ancestors, contained in the works that comprise the Kabbalah. Although later research has proved that this was in fact written in Spain in the thirteenth century (there are references to the Crusades within it), tradition holds that it is wisdom passed by God to Adam and through successive generations until the second century AD when it was written down. The knowledge contained in the Kabbalah deals with the nature of God, angels and man. According to the tradition, God works through ten intelligences or emanations, nine of which stem from the first – the wish to be manifest. The nine are also grouped together in threes, each three influencing one sphere of man's activity and one area of the body. The first three emanations – crown, wisdom and intelligence – influence the intellectual sphere and rule the

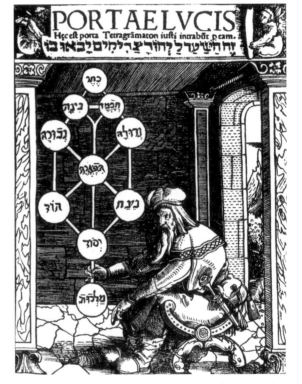

head; love, justice and beauty influence the moral sphere and the arms; strength, splendour and foundation are concerned with the physical sphere and the legs. The final emanation, kingdom, binds together and surrounds these three groups of three.

According to the Kabbalah there are four worlds. The first is the world of emanations, where the souls of men exist. All men must come to earth to fulfil the destiny decreed for them or reach the potential that exists within them. Those who fail must return three times in order to be sufficiently pure to re-enter the world of emanations. From this world pro-

Opposite page: In 'Entry into the Spirit World' Dario Poli shows the pure brightness of the spirit world protected, at its entrance, by a spirit guardian. As a result of his deep understanding of the ancient mystical rites, Nostradamus was able to gain access to, and communicate with, its spirit inhabitants.

Left: Jewish Kabbalist holding the Tree of Life, a mystical diagram made up of 10 spheres interconnected by 22 paths (corresponding to the 22 letters of the Hebrew alphabet). The Kabbalist multiplied the 32 resulting paths with the four 'worlds' in order to enter and describe the secret and mystical parts of the universe.

Right: Born in Greece in the fifth century BC, Pythagoras was both a philosopher and mathematician. The Pythagorean theorem for right-angled triangles has been attributed to him although this and other findings were probably discovered later by the Pythagorean School. This depiction of Pythagoras is from a medieval manuscript.

ceeds the world of creations, from that the world of formations (which is the home of the angels), from that the world of action, home of the evil spirits.

The Kabbalah itself says that all the doctrines it describes are contained in the Hebrew scriptures, but that only the initiated (those of a spiritual disposition) can perceive them. Of most importance to the medieval magicians was the Kabbalah's emphasis on the virtues of names and numbers. The initiated would be able to find those verses of the Hebrew scriptures which had special significance and work with them to find their hidden meanings. Verses might be set one above another and new words created by reading the lines downward. Or texts might be arranged in a square and read in a different configuration. The last or first letters of the words of a particular verse might be taken and used to form new words and new meanings. Finally, each letter within

the Kabbalah had a numerical value. A word, or combination of letters, adds up to a numerical total which is the same as that for a different word or combination of letters. And there is one of the simplest cipher codes of all, in which a represents l, b, m and so on.

As a Renaissance scholar Nostradamus sought out ancient texts that described ways of raising the level of human consciousness to a more advanced state. But as a product of a period only gradually learning how to flex its intellectual muscle, he had one foot still very firmly planted in the Middle Ages. He was not alone. Despite the thirst for new knowledge, particularly about the nature of humanity and its place in the universe, there was also a strand of what might be termed 'scientific magic', an interest in all ways of explaining the unexplainable. The renewed interest in Pythagoras, the Greek mathematician of the sixth century BC, led some scholars to regard mathematical

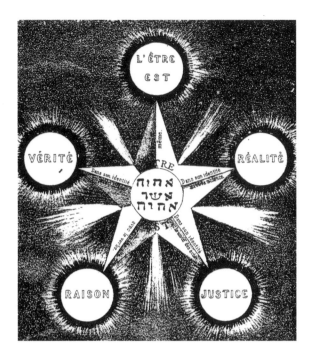

symbols and geometric formulae as possibly holding clues to the secrets of the universe. Looking again at the classics led to a reappraisal of the roles of the sibyls and prophets of ancient times. Both these strands of enquiry appear to have been sanctioned – or at least ignored – by the Church. The works of the Greek scholar Hermes Trismegistus (reputed to be the scribe of the gods and therefore the author of all sacred texts), which were translated into Latin in 1471, were also widely circulated and said to hold the key to concealed knowledge. And there was a widespread belief that by making a representation of a spiritual pattern, such as a pentagram, on earth, its deeper significance would be revealed.

The practice of magic has been a part of every culture since prehistoric times (magical practices have been discerned in cave paintings), but the birthplace of what might be termed a systematic magical tradition was in the temples of Egypt (according to the Kabbalah, this stems from the time of the Jewish exile in Egypt) thousands of years before Christ was born. It was here that temple priests formulated the mystical practices which formed the basis of a relationship between the individual and the gods of the Egyptian pantheon. Practices such as the memorizing of formulas and spells, in addition to tests of courage and honour prepared the individual, so long as he possessed a highly developed moral character, for an introduction to secret knowledge and ultimate entry into deeper layers of divine consciousness.

Pythagoras and other early philosophers who travelled to Egypt carried these mysteries back to Greece. In the fourth century the Neoplatonists continued these mystical traditions in the belief that the truth about man's existence can be reached through 'rising above' mortal desires, therefore becoming more godlike. The murder of their leader, protesting at the exclusivity and militancy of Christianity, by an enraged mob of Christian monks in AD

415 spelled the end of the philosophical tolerance of magic and drove these mystical practices underground for six centuries. During the Middle Ages the description and publication of these forbidden arts were condemned by the Church which feared that people might become inspired by them. The Inquisition condemned to the stake on grounds of heresy all those who practised magic.

During the Renaissance the influence of magic gained new strength. Many people inquired into wisdom that was formerly forbid-

Magical diagrams such as the Pentagram of the Absolute *(left)* and the magical square *(below)* have been used by most secret and occult societies through the ages. The geometric designs, representing the mysteries of deity and creation, were supposed to be of special virtue in rites of evocation and conjuration. The Pentagram, in particular, was considered to be extremely powerful, due to its shape. With one point in the ascendant, it signified Christ; with two points in the ascendant it signified Satan. Hence it could be used to evoke the powers of both light and darkness.

Right: Engraved on the facade of the Notre Dame cathedral in Paris are six symbols representing six secret processes of alchemy. The symbols decorate the shields held by the women. Alchemists devised many secret signs for the materials with which they worked in order to preserve the esoteric nature of their practices.

den. Printing presses, ceaselessly producing Bibles and the ancient classics, were also producing other works, some savouring strongly of magic but others pushing the frontiers of knowledge. Although the *Index* listed books banned or restricted for various reasons (Protestant tracts in a Catholic state, anything slightly risqué, and so on), in many parts of Europe a determined scholar with sufficient money and discretion could probably read more or less what he chose. Some printers seem to have had the sixteenth-century equivalent of a mailing list of clients known to be interested in a particular subject, and the Inquisitors could not keep track of everyone. However, the superstitious beliefs of centuries still pervaded most aspects of thinking and behaviour and continued to do so until the introduction of nineteenth-century scientific method established bodies of factual knowledge capable of proof.

One of the perennial concerns of magicians was the transmutation of base metals into gold by a formula which originated in ancient Egypt. Alchemy, the science which developed from this preoccupation and laid the foundations of the science of chemistry – the first practical chemistry book, published in 1597 by the German Libavanus, was entitled *Alchemia* – was also concerned with prolonging life and, more importantly, with generating life. Small wonder, then, that the Church was concerned with this branch of magic.

Nostradamus certainly dabbled in alchemy; he admits as much in the Preface to the first edition of the *Centuries*, written in the form of a letter to his infant son César: '... that henceforth you might not be abused in the search of the perfect transformation, as much lunar as solar, and to seek in the waters uncorruptible metal, I have burnt them [the books on alchemy] all to ashes.'

In the Preface, too, Nostradamus names certain records of ancient traditions of occult

Left: This portrait of Iamblichus is from Jacques Bossard's *De Divinatione et Magicis*. Iamblichus was a fourth-century Syrian philosopher who stressed the importance of certain virtues by which humans could obtain ecstatic union with the One, who exists outside the scope of human understanding. He was known as 'the divine' or 'the inspirer'.

and ritual magic. They include *The Keys of Solomon* (supposedly written by Solomon, although almost certainly written in the fourteenth or fifteenth century and concerned with finding treasure and altering the free will of others) and *De Mysteriis Ægyptorum*, by Iamblichus, the fourth-century philosopher. Both these works were forbidden by the Church, but they were almost certainly consulted by the prophet.

The similarity between Iamblichus's description of the preparations necessary for a consultation with the oracle at Delphi and Nostradamus's own description in the first two quatrains of the first century (see page 32) are too similar to be coincidence. At Delphi, in a bower of laurels (later a temple) erected over a steaming fissure in the rocks from which the answers to questions concerning the future emanated, a young girl, the chosen intermediary between the gods and the questioner, sat on a tripod made of brass. Before the consultation, she washed, drank sacred waters and chewed a laurel leaf. She was wearing a laurel crown. As

SIBYLLA.

she asked a question she peered into the steam. She was often in a trance-like state and in many cases her words were garbled and incoherent and the priests at the shrine had to interpret them for the public. According to Nostradamus, when the moment of illumination came through the 'slender flame', he was in an inspired mental state, as if in a trance. Trance induction in classical times was a respected method of obtaining valid prophecies; it is also used today in modern witch cults. Drum-beating, chanting and hallucinogenic drugs such as mescaline also induce altered states of consciousness whereby everyday reality is exchanged for intense and heightened experience.

Nostradamus would have been unable to forget that the Inquisition forbade the practice of magic; the likely punishment was torture and (or torture to) death. Anxious to conceal

the nature of his activities, he claimed in the letter–Preface that those books he had read were not forbidden: 'Although this occult philosophy was not forbidden, I could never be persuaded to meddle with it, although many volumes ... were presented to me.' He continues by saying that he did in fact read these books, but afterward burned them: 'fearing what might happen, after I had read them, I presented them to Vulcan and, while he was devouring them, the flame mixed with the air, there was an unwonted light more bright than the usual flame and it was as if there were lightning, shining all the house over, as if it had been all in flame'. He also warns his son against the practice of forbidden magic: 'I caution you against the vanity of the execrable magic forbidden by the Sacred Scriptures and by the Canons of the Church; though we have to exempt judicial astrology, by which and by means of divine inspiration, with continual calculations, we have put in writing, our prophecies.'

So what exactly was the nature of the prophetic experience in the attic room? One of the many aspects of the Kabbalah is its espousal of intensive meditation to penetrate deep layers of consciousness. Perhaps Nostradamus used meditation. It is probable that he used astrological calculations to select a propitious date and time to prophesy, that he consulted his occult books to perfect the details of his ritual, and that once all his instruments were in place he concentrated his mind on gazing into the bowl of water on the brass tripod. Perhaps he used incantations to focus his mind.

As to whether Nostradamus was a magician, one scene may answer the question. It is recorded that in the privacy of Catherine's apartments, on his first visit to court, Nostradamus showed her the fates of her children as they passed round a room into which she could see, as if she were looking through a window or seeing in a mirror. First was Francis II (see page 36) who walked once round the room and vanished (he was king for little more than year). Charles IX circled the room fourteen times – an indication that he would rule for fourteen years. Charles's fourteen-year reign (1560–74) was dominated by his mother. Henri III circled the room fifteen times. Henri ascended the throne in 1574 and his reign was cut short by his assassination in 1589. François, Duke of Alencon, faded into Henri of Navarre, who ascended the throne in 1589 as Henri IV, the first Bourbon king. Catherine is believed to have been so shaken by and believing of this scene that she married her daughter to Henri of Navarre, for if her son could not be king then her daughter could definitely be queen.

If Catherine did indeed 'see' her children, then Nostradamus must have worked something that, by today's standards at least, would have to be called 'magic'.

Left: In the reflection of his magic mirror Nostradamus revealed the fate of each of Catherine de Medici's children.

CELESTIAL SCIENTIST

'If thou livest the natural age of man thou shalt see in thy climate, and under the Heavens of thy nativity, the future things that have been foretold.'
Preface to the first edition of the *Centuries*, 1555

ASTROLOGY – the study of the movement and positions of the heavenly bodies in relation to their presumed influence on human affairs – was a respected profession in the sixteenth century. Most scientists, doctors and scholars knew the rudiments of astrology even if they did not openly practise the science. Rather than the flowering of Renaissance knowledge depressing the popularity of astrology, it increased it. The reappraisal of classical texts brought the planetary gods to life for a new generation of scholars. Venus, goddess of love and fertility, Saturn, father of the gods, and Mars, god of war, assumed a new reality. And, perhaps surprisingly, astrology did not attract the disapproval of the Church. Astrologers were not influencing what was going to happen, or interfering with free will, merely offering an opinion on when future events would occur.

Until the sixteenth century, the sciences of astrology and astronomy – the study of the celestial bodies themselves – were far more closely aligned that they are considered today, and certainly Nostradamus learned both from his grandfather Jean de St Rémy. It was only with the work of Copernicus (see page 16), who revised Ptolemy's astrological tables, and the Dane, Tycho Brahe (1546–1601) that the two disciplines were separated. Equally, every astronomical or astrological chart relied on naked-eye observations of the stars and planets and mathematical calculations. The first telescope was not built until 1608.

Astrological tradition proposes twelve houses, each with its own special characteristics which are imparted to those born under that sign. The twelve signs are also grouped

Opposite page: Love is depicted under the influence of Venus and Taurus from a fifteenth century manuscript. Venus is the ancient Roman goddess of Love, while Taurus, the second sign of the zodiac, governs the period from 20th April to 20th May. This is a time of rebirth in the natural world when, traditionally, lovers meet out of doors to celebrate the spirit of spring.

Left: The Danish astronomer Tycho Brahe produced a comprehensive study of the solar system and pinpointed the accurate positions of more than 750 fixed stars. His observations were the most accurate possible before the invention of the telescope.

according to the four elements – earth, air, fire and water, each of which also has its effect on the character.

The aspects of the planets are even more important than those of the houses since they act on an hour-by-hour basis. The degree of difference between the positions of two planets, either at the hour of an individual's birth or at the hour that a question is asked, is also important in drawing a horoscope, which is technically defined as a prediction of the future for an individual.

There is a tradition that astrology was practised in ancient Chaldea more than 5000 years ago. In these ancient times the stars came to be regarded as supreme gods whose movement across the sky determined the events of this world. The unfathomable heavens, it was believed, were inhabited with heroes and demons irreconcilably at odds with each other, and their perpetual strife was reflected in the affairs of individuals on earth. The origins of the specific attributes of the stars are unclear. In the case of Venus, for example, they were derived from appearance. The brightest of all the planets glowed red in the night sky and was unquestionably a symbol of love and sexual desire. But in most instances the characteristics given to the stars were inspired by myth and legend and had no basis in observed phenomena. The seven known planets were themselves deities and worshipped or feared for the attributes which have historically become associated with them – love, aggression, speed, melancholy and so on.

Although some astrological and prophetic arts are reputed to have been handed down from even earlier civilizations which succeeded in passing on their skills and knowledge before they became extinct, it is likely that it was the Babylonian and Assyrian forms of the science (set down in Cicero's *De Divinatione*, written during the first century BC) that reached Egypt. From there astrological study spread to Greece, Persia, India and the Far East. The fundamental basis of astrology as we know it today is a development of the earliest beliefs of corresponding influences between heaven and earth. The Greeks perfected their own intuitive perception of correspondence into an understanding of the cosmos as one huge and interconnected life force whose various facets were reflected elsewhere in the universe at any given time. They believed that at birth an intelligible picture of a life and personality was created according to the conjunction of the stars. This astral connection was reinforced by the occult belief that universal events were cyclical and that existence, having no beginning and no end, was an everlasting continuum.

Below: The Medieval preoccupation with horoscopes is typified here by this illustration of a woman in the throes of labour, attended by her midwives as an astrologer calmly plots a birthchart for the new baby at the window behind her.

After the Roman era, astrology lost popularity and was not revived until the ninth century when serious studies were made by the Arabs. The astronomical works of Ptolemy, the Egyptian scholar of the second century AD, were translated in Arabic, under the title *Almagest*, and reached Spain from the Middle East. By the time of Nostradamus, astrology was probably at the peak of its popularity. It touched everyone (this was one of the major reasons for the success of Nostradamus's and others' almanacs), but inevitably the concerns of the farmer who wanted to know whether to plant his fields this week or next (natural astrology deals with the operation of the stars on the natural world) were held to be inferior to those of the king, who might want to know if it was a propitious time to wage war (judicial astrology is the branch of the science dealing with the futures of individuals and nations – it was the study of judicial astrology that attracted future biographer Chavigny to seek Nostradamus as his teacher).

Not much is known of Nostradamus the astrologer during his years of medical study and life as an itinerant doctor. It seems likely,

Above: 'Astrological Study'. In this extraordinary drawing, Dario Poli attempts to show the link between astrology, the psychic world and the confusion of human existence. Nostradamus tried to make sense of this confusion through his study of astrology.

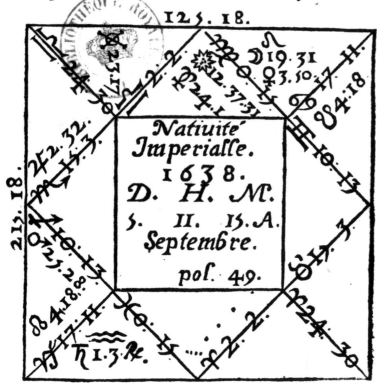

L'HOROSCOPE
IMPERIAL
DE
LOVIS XIV.
DIEV-DONNE'.

Predit par l'Oracle François & Michel Nostradamus.

Natiuité Imperialle.
1638.
D. H. M.
5. II. 15. A.
Septembre.
pol. 49.

Et se vend

A PARIS,

Chez **FRANÇOIS HVART,** à la Montagne Ste Geneviève
proche l'Espée de bois.

M. DC. LII.

Above: The horoscope of King Louis XIV from a 1652 edition of the *Centuries,* by Nostradamus.

Medici in 1556, he reached the grander realms of judicial astrology. Nostradamus spent much of that visit casting horoscopes for courtiers and for visiting dignitaries who paid him handsomely for his services.

Ambitious and educated, Catherine was fascinated with the occult and with astrology. Convinced as early as the age of twelve, when she left Florence for France to marry Henri II, that she would found a great dynasty, she relied increasingly on Nostradamus's visions of her future. She was not the only monarch to have her own astrologer. Queen Elizabeth I of England regularly consulted the astrologer and occultist, John Dee (1527–1608). Dee's visions were different from those of Nostradamus in that, while Dee claimed to see spirits and talk with them, he could not remember what they had said at the time of his visions. He therefore worked with an assistant (for much of the time one Edward Kelley who seems to have duped Dee into believing that he was seeing what Dee may have suggested to him was there) who talked to the spirits while Dee transcribed the conversations. Elizabeth is also said to have

however, that he used his knowledge of astrology to judge the most favourable time to administer his treatments. Once settled in Salon, he was able to install a small observatory at the top of his house and spend long hours at his favourite pastime. He 'served his apprenticeship' with the somewhat mundane natural astrological concerns of the citizens of Salon. With his summons to court by Catherine de

Left: Elizabeth I (1533-1603) was queen during a period in which England became a major European power in politics, commerce and the arts. Elizabeth's claim to the throne was threatened by Mary Queen of Scots, based on the questionable legality of Elizabeth's father, Henry VIII,s second marriage to Anne Boleyn (Elizabeth's mother). The portrait is by Nicholas Hilliard.

consulted Dee on the significance of the appearance of any new star or comet in the night sky. There were also astrologers in residence at the courts of, among others, Florence and Bohemia. The uniqueness of Nostradamus is that his knowledge of the stars and their influence was only one of a number of varied and interconnected talents.

And what of the horoscope of Nostradamus himself? He was born in the Piscean age, under the influence of Jupiter. It was an age of miracles and of unquestioning acceptance of God's purpose. A belief in magic and the supernatural was at the very foundation of life during this period which is reputed to last 1,500 years, from approximately 950 BC to AD 2050. But the age was slowly moving out of Pisces into the cusp with Aquarius, whose dominant planet was Saturn. The thrust of the changes occurring during this transition will last from Nostradamus's own time to the end of the twentieth century. Gradually the Aquarian age will lead mankind away from a blind belief in supernatural powers as a cornerstone of its existence to a more reasoned approach where nothing at all is unquestionable or beyond the power of scientific investigation. The Renaissance, of which Nostradamus was undoubtedly a part, occurred exactly at this time of flux and change.

Opposite page: Doctor Dee with his seer, Edward Kelley, is shown here demonstrating his skills for Guy Fawkes. Dr John Dee was court astrologer to Mary Tudor before practising astrology at the court of Elizabeth I. He was asked to name a propitious day for her coronation and gave Elizabeth lessons in the mystical interpretation of his writings.

The May Cherry
Rise 2

COSMETICIAN AND RECIPE WRITER

I S IT POSSIBLE FOR RENOWNED scholarship, extraordinary medical skills and a prophetic ability which has survived more than 400 years to be combined with a talent for making cosmetics, skin creams, love potions and jam? Nostradamus, least well known today for these latter accomplishments but patronized by the rich and famous of his day for his cosmetic and culinary skills, has proved that it is. It is apparent from his first full-length book, *Traité des Fardemens* (*farder* means 'to rouge' or 'to put on make up') published in 1552 and reprinted in 1555, that Nostradamus had a great flair for selecting and combining ingredients for these purposes.

His skill in this area probably derived from two main sources – his dabblings in alchemy, and the knowledge gleaned from his contacts and dealings with apothecaries during his years as a doctor. The first part of the *Traité* contains a variety of potions and pomades (or ointments) for whitening the skin and removing blemishes; tinctures to sweeten and scent the breath, and whiten the teeth; soap to soften the hands; and lotions to give hair the appearance of spun gold or black jet, or to restore the original colour of the hair. In the second part of the book which has a culinary flavour, Nostradamus records his recipes for jams and preserves, dwelling on both their visual appearance and their 'sovereign' quality. Both types of products seem to have been in great demand and must, presumably, have bought the prophet substantial financial rewards.

Opposite page: The May Cherry from *Tradescant's Orchard* – a collection of early seventeenth century paintings of English fruit trees.

Left: Cosmeticians compounding a Balsam. Balsam is the aromatic resinous substance that flows spontaneously from an incision in a plant. It was used in medicinal preparations and perfumery as well as in the making of incense. Heating in a furnace made the balsam more fluid, after which it was often mixed with essential oils.

Above: A mortar and pestle were among the most important culinary utensils used for preparing pastes and other finely ground elements of cuisine. This elaborately carved example dates from the fifteenth century.

Right: This detail of a young girl from a fifteenth century manuscript exemplifies the medieval ideal of beauty, which stressed the importance of a fair skin. Women used all kinds of cosmetic preparations in order to stimulate and improve their complexions.

believed that creams bought from Nostradamus contained magic ingredients that would make them irresistible.

One of Nostradamus's face creams, recommended to maintain a youthful skin, is as interesting for the description of its effects as for its recipe and constituents which, regardless of short-term benefit, in the light of modern knowledge may have caused long-term damage to the skin. The potion was made with successive grindings, boilings and distillation of the ingredients and Nostradamus recommended washing the face with the resulting paste in the morning before leaving home. Its main purpose was to preserve and whiten the face, thereby maintaining the beauty of a woman until the age of sixty provided she used it properly and regularly (white skin was one of the major prerequisites of a beautiful woman: suntanned skin suggested outdoor manual labour and, as such, was not to be desired). Nostradamus believed that all women, espe-

The book itself was written 'at the request of a great princess ... by means of her very illustrious magnificence'. She may have been of a 'certain age', not wishing to reveal either her beauty secrets or the fact that she resorted to artifice to maintain her appearance. The period during which Nostradamus was engaged in making these products and setting down their recipes coincided with the period of his greatest prophetic inspiration. Perhaps he found the life of cook and cosmetician a relaxing contrast to his more intellectual pursuits. The success of his preparations ensured a steady stream of customers: beautiful young girls wanting make-up and the means to make their lovers vigorous and strong; and the old or ugly who

cially those who had had many children (a common occurrence in an era when between one-third and one-half of all children born failed to make it past infancy and birth control was unheard of), deteriorated by five per cent a year – an observation which, even taking into account the vicissitudes of sixteenth-century life, seems rather harsh.

FACE CREAM

4 lemons in quarters

an ecu's weight of quicksilver [mercury, which is toxic]

½ lb Venetian white lead [also toxic, though widely used in cosmetics until the nineteenth century]

6 eggs

spring water

The potion prepared by Nostradamus to ensnare a member of the opposite sex was an ancient love philtre called *poculum amatorium ad Venerem* reputed to have been invented by Medea, the Greek sorceress deserted by Jason after she had helped him to steal the Golden Fleece. The potion was used, in the words of the prophet–cosmetician, 'for the deed of love'. He extolled its extraordinary virtues, saying that it was so strong and effective: 'that if a man has a little of it in his mouth ... as he kisses a woman, or the woman him, and discharges it mixed with saliva and puts it into the other's mouth, this will suddenly create a fire in her ... but her heart breaks to achieve the amorous purpose, and not with any other person than he or she who gives the kiss ... and the love of these two people remains so inviolable and for so long that neither one nor the other can survive without being together.'

Left: The mandrake plant, as conceived in a fifteenth century book on plants and health, had a forked root thought to resemble the human form. In medieval times it was believed that as the mandrake was pulled from the ground it uttered a shriek that could kill or derange all those who did not block their ears against it.

POCULUM AMATORIUM AD VENEREM

1 Pick 3 mandrake fruits at sunrise, wrap them in vervain leaves and wild garlic, and leave them exposed to the dew until the following morning. [Mandrake is a herb whose thick, forked root resembles a human body; it has long been believed to have healing and aphrodisiac properties.]

2 Then take 6 grains of *lapis magneticus* or lover's stone, grind it on marble and sprinkle on it some of the juice from the mandrake fruit.

3 Collect the blood of seven male sparrows, bled through the left wing.

4 Bring together enough ambergris to equal the weight of 57 grains of barley; 7 grains of musk; enough of the best cinnamon to equal 370 grains of barley; enough cloves and wood aloes to equal the weight of three pence; an eyelet of each part of the devilfish, soaked in money to equal the weight of 21 grains; and 500 grains of *racina apurisis*. [Ambergris is a waxy, musk-scented substance found in the intestines of sperm whales; devilfish was a generic word for several large fish.]

5 Add some wine from Crete, twice as much in weight as all the previous ingredients. Finally add 700 grains of very fine sugar (a little more than one ounce).

6 Grind and macerate everything in a marble mortar with a wooden pestle, then gather it up in a silver spoon and place it in a glass vessel and boil it on the fire until the sugar has turned into a syrup or julep.

7 Squeeze or press the liquid into a vessel of glass, silver or gold.

8 To use, put a piece weighing half an ecu in the mouth. In Nostradamus's words: 'It is simple enough.'

When Nostradamus was in Avignon during his first period of travelling he visited the papal legate with a gift of quince jelly, a speciality of which he was particularly proud. He describes it as '*d'une soveraine beauté, bonté, saveur et excellence*' (supreme in appearance, goodness and taste). Nostradamus awarded it the additional accolade of being fit to present to a king and is said to have made a gift of this homemade quince jelly to King Henri II on one of his visits to the French court.

According to Nostradamus the best jams and preserves came from the Levant and from Valencia, although those from Venice and Genoa were almost as good. The most popular preserve in sixteenth-century France was made with the peel or flesh of lemon with sugar, but Nostradamus selects several other preserves for special note in the *Traité*. They include oranges with sugar and honey preserved in such a way that they were as good to eat after a day as if they had been soaking for two weeks; sweet cherries, called amarenes by the Italians, either in pieces or in jelly; and ginger which was considered suitable for cold women who could not conceive and even more effective for men who were unable 'to perform their natural duty' (presumably ginger's reputation as an improver of the circulation was responsible for this 'remedy'). Another recipe which Nostradamus seemed to have had a particular taste for and which he gives, *con amore* (with love), was a preserve of little green lemons and oranges boiled with the tenderest green buds and shoots which the tree produced. Lettuce preserve – a truly imaginative way of treating the stalwart of the green salad – was made with the stalk only of the lettuce which was picked when the plant had gone to seed and boiled with its own weight of sugar and water. Perhaps it is appropriate for Nostradamus's final recipe to be for his favourite cherry jelly, 'as clear and vermillion as a fine ruby' and which is made 'by adding nothing but the fruit'.

Right: Title page from Arnaldus de Villanova's *Régime de Santé pour conserver le corps humain* – a French book on health published in Paris in 1532.

CHERRY JELLY

1 Take as many as you wish of the finest and ripest sweet cherries you can find and remove the stalks. Put the cherries in a sieve or flour sifter with an earthenware dish beneath it to catch the juices (copper, brass or tin dishes spoil the goodness and colour of the juice).

2 Put some powdered sugar into the dish. If there is no sugar in the dish, the juice will curdle; the sugar absorbs the juice and takes on its taste and colour.

3 When all the juice has passed through the sieve and only the pits and skins remain, pour everything into a saucepan, place the saucepan over a charcoal fire, and bring it to the boil. Carefully remove the scum that rises to the top with a perforated spoon until there is no more scum left.

4 When the mixture is cooked, transfer it into small, shallow pots and leave to cool. When you look at the pots in daylight or lamp-light they should be 'lovely as a ruby'.

Note: To make a jelly 'which is fine and good in all perfection', Nostradamus suggests using a small quantity of sugar and a large amount of cherries, so that they set more easily.

Left: The Tradescant Cherry from *Tradescant's Orchard.* The cherry preserve that most delighted Nostradamus for its flavour and wonderful ruby colour was made from his own recipe.

OLD AGE, DEATH AND LEGACY

A S EARLY AS HIS FIRST visit to court in 1556, Nostradamus – by that time in his fifties – was plagued by arthritic gout. Although in the sixteenth century, the word 'gout' was used for almost any condition involving swollen joints, there is little doubt that the nature of Nostradamus's illness made movement difficult and he frequently had to take to his bed.

His connections at court and his fame meant wealth and financial security, but particularly after Henri II's death in 1559, the nature of his powers aroused suspicion, not only among the people of Paris, but also among the people of Salon. In that year his house was pelted with stones by local *cabans*, or peasants. Fearful for his family's safety he found refuge for them in the town jail until things quietened down. The peasants' suspicions were understandable: what kind of man manufactured drugs and potions for handsome profits, could predict the death of the king with an astonishing degree of accuracy and had an attic room where the flame of a candle burned late into the night?

Nostradamus's increasing mobility problems were one reason why, in 1564, in the

Opposite page: 'Final Years'. Here Dario Poli interprets Nostradamus's vision of Mars, the god of war gazing down on the wilful destruction by human beings of their own world.

Left: A ball at the court of King Henri III of France (French School). Henri was Catherine's favourite son and the last of the Valois line. During the French Wars of Religion, Henri continued to fight against the Huguenots although just before he died (childless), he acknowledged Henri of Navarre, the Huguenot leader, as his heir.

course of a two-year-long 'progress' through France (in effect a giant public relations exercise which was to terminate at the Spanish border), Catherine de Medici chose to call on her court astrologer, perhaps also showing her continued solidarity with the prophet. By this time acting as regent for her second son, the fourteen-year-old Charles IX, Catherine was trying to prevent civil war. Increasing tension between Catholics and Huguenots had resulted in the first conflict between the factions in 1562. (Charles and Catherine presided over the St Bartholomew's Day massacre in 1572, the bloodiest event of the Wars, in which 3000 Huguenots died.) It is likely that Catherine was encouraged by Nostradamus's prediction that all her sons would be kings and convinced, therefore, that the Huguenots were unlikely to be the ultimate victors in the wars.

Plague had recently struck Salon with the result that many of the town's inhabitants had fled, leaving too few people to give the 800-strong royal party a welcome Charles felt

Below: An engraving from 1600 depicting the Massacre of St Bartholomew in 1572, the most notorious incident of the Wars of Religion. On the orders of Charles IX, almost all the leading Huguenots in Paris were murdered, along with thousands more throughout the rest of France.

appropriate for a king. He ordered the town's citizens to return or suffer the consequences. The citizens obeyed since, by all accounts a vicious bully, Charles was not a monarch to cross: he was reputed to heighten the pleasures of the hunt by decapitating wild pigs with his sword. Having engineered a fitting welcome, Charles and the rest of the entourage arrived in Salon on 17th October. Charles wore a purple cloak with silver trimmings, and amethyst earrings adorned his ears. He rode an African horse with grey trappings and black velvet harness with gold fringes. The streets had been strewn with sand and branches of sweet-smelling rosemary, and a dais was erected on which the town's dignitaries had gathered to greet him. His first words were 'I have come to see Nostradamus.'

The prophet was presented to the king who gave him the title 'counsellor' and appointed him his physician in ordinary, a post which was accompanied by a salary and other financial benefits. Nostradamus took this moment to

complain to the king of the way he had been treated by some of the townsfolk, an indication of his resentment toward his fellow citizens. Catherine wished to see his wife and family and asked Nostradamus to draw up the horoscope of her youngest son, Edward of Anjou who, as Henri III, was to be the last of the Valois kings.

There was one thing that Nostradamus did not tell Catherine. He was anxious to see a young page in the royal entourage, Henri of Navarre, Charles's cousin. Henri refused to allow Nostradamus to see him undressed, although the prophet merely wished to confirm his belief that the young boy would one day be king. And this, according to astrological practice, could be achieved by identifying the position of moles on the body. The following morning Nostradamus managed to be present in Henri's bedchamber and saw him rising from his bed. He instantly confirmed his prediction, which was fulfilled in 1589 when Henri of Navarre took the French throne as Henri IV, ending the Wars of Religion. Under his authority in 1598, the Edict of Nantes allowed freedom of worship in France.

After visiting Catherine's daughter in Spain, Charles and Catherine travelled to Salon to see Nostradamus on their return journey. On this

occasion they visited his home, met his wife and children and gave him a gift of 300 gold crowns. It was the last meeting of the queen and prophet. At the end of June 1566, the gout turned to dropsy (oedema) and he sent for the local Franciscan friar to hear his confession and administer the last rites. On 2nd July, just before sunrise, the dropsy suffocated him.

The circumstances of Nostradamus's death were recorded by his disciple and biographer, Chavigny. According to him, Nostradamus knew the day and hour he would die and frequently reminded him of the note he had

Above: Charles IX and Catherine de Medici on the Eve of St Bartholomew in Paris in 1572.

Left: The sword of Henri IV (formerly Henri of Navarre) is kissed by Pedro de Toledo, ambassador to Philip II of Spain. King Philip II was the last in a line of men to challenge Henri's right to the French throne, but without success. Painting by J.A.D. Ingres.

written only a short time before in a friend's almanac, 'Hic prope mors est' – 'My death is near'. The day before his death the pair spent many hours together, not parting until late at night when Nostradamus said, 'You will not see me alive at sunrise.' He had also predicted his death in one of his prophetic verses:

> Du retour d'Ambassade do de Roy mis au lieu
> Plus n'en serea: sera alle a DIEU
> Parans plus proche, amis, freres du sang.
> Trouve tant mort pres du lict & du banc
> PRÉSAGE CXLI

> Returning from the mission, the king's gift put
> away,
> There was nothing more to do but render the
> soul to God;
> His nearest relatives, brothers and friends
> Would find him dead on the bed seated on the
> bench nearby.

Nostradamus had given much thought to the matter of his death. On 17th June he called in a local notary to draw up his last will and testament. He left the large sum of 3,444 crowns in addition to his personal possessions; family arguments may have prompted the codicil added a few days later leaving special items to his eldest son and daughter. So great was Nostradamus's resentment at the way he had been treated by the people of Salon that he left

instructions that he was to be interred upright so that their feet should not trample over him in death. His coffin was duly immured in the wall of the church of the Franciscan friars in Salon, above which his wife erected a marble tablet engraved with his likeness and with the following epitaph, in imitation of the Roman historian Livy.

> Here lie the bones of the most illustrious Michel
> Nostradamus
> The only one, in the judgment of all mortals,
> worthy to write with a pen almost divine,
> under the influence of the stars, of the future
> events of the entire world.
> He lived sixty-two years six months and
> seventeen days.
> He died in Salon in the year 1566
> Let posterity trouble not his repose.

Nostradamus must have foreseen interference with his tomb and warned: 'The man who opens the tomb when it is found and does not

Right: Church gateway at Salon.

Far right: Engraving of Nostradamus in eighteenth century romantic style.

close it at once will meet evil that no one will be able to prove ....' In 1700 the municipal authorities of Salon decided to renovate the vertical tomb and, intrigued by the warning, could not resist opening the coffin and having look inside. Around the neck of his skeleton hung a medallion inscribed with the date 1700. The lid was quickly replaced.

Nearly 100 years later, during the French Revolution, a drunken contingent of National Guards from Marseilles rampaged through Salon and descended on the church where the body of Nostradamus rested. Remembering an old superstition that anyone who drank blood from the skull of Nostradamus would receive his psychic powers, they hacked through the

marble slabs that protected his tomb, opened the coffin and cast the bones of his skeleton around the church. One guard filled his skull with wine and drank from it. The mayor of Salon rushed to the church and frightened the desecrators by reminding them of Nostradamus's warning. The next day the bones of the prophet were assembled and the body reinterred.

That evening the same guards were ambushed by Royalist soldiers on their way to Marseilles; the guard who had drunk from the skull was found shot through the head.

As he had predicted the manner of his death, so Nostradamus foresaw recognition for his prophecies.

De cinq cent ans plus compte l'on tiendra
Celui qu'estoit l'adornement de son temps:
Puis à un coup grand clarté donra,
Que par ce siecle les rendra tres contens.
CIII Q94

For five hundred years more they will take no
*   notice*
Of him who was the ornament of his time,
Then suddenly a great revelation will be made.
That will make the people of that age most
*   happy.*

There is a conviction in the words of this quatrain rarely found in other parts of the *Centuries*. Not only is Nostradamus certain that

the inspired nature of his prophecies will be recognized, but he is also able to date precisely when this revelation will occur. Some 500 years after the publication of the first edition of his works, that is in the year 2055, something momentous will happen to make people believe in the validity of his prophecies. This would seem likely to occur during the period of peace immediately following the 27-year-long Third World War, due to end in the year 2026 (see pages 134–7). Although the tone of the quatrain is highly self-congratulatory, there is little doubt that, even without his prophecies, Nostradamus would have been 'an ornament of his time'. It seems that for him the rewards of

Right: French cartoon of Nostradamus, 1790. Images of Nostradamus range from the realistic to the imaginary, and humorous to the more sinister.

years of disciplined study and prophetic output lay in the belief that his gift of prophecy would eventually bring contentment to people through a revealed understanding of his work.

Much of what is known about Nostradamus today derives from the first-hand biography *La Vie et le Testament de Michel Nostradamus* written by Chavigny and published in 1594. Given the controversial nature of the prophecies and the fame that they achieved from their first publication, the *Centuries* have been forged many times over their 400-year lifespan, and some of these misrepresentations have given the prophet a bad name.

It is not known exactly how many early editions of the Nostradamus's works are still in existence. The difficulty with the *Centuries* in particular is that they were published in two parts, in 1555 and 1568. Several of the earliest editions are undated and some 'counterfeit' editions, altered copies of the original text, were printed about 100 years after their stated dates of publication. (An edition published in Paris in 1649, and falsely dated 1568, contained forged quatrains against Cardinal Mazarin, for example.)

The *Centuries* has been in print since its first publication, although the number of commentaries and new editions has varied over the years. Interest in Nostradamus at certain periods, notably during the French Revolution and the Second World War, has given rise to new editions of the *Centuries* and more publications about the prophet. A proportion of these books have contained blatant alterations to the original texts to suit their authors' biased readings of the original; this has had the effect of 'arming' Nostradamus's detractors. And there are the genuinely sceptical and critical who choose to concentrate on the unintelligible prophecies or those which, with hindsight, were wrong.

In spite of these setbacks, the stunning accu-

racy of so many of the predictions has ensured the survival of the work and the reputation of its author into the twenty-first century.

Above: So successful were Nostradamus's almanacs in his lifetime that even after his death various predictive works were attributed to him. As Nostradamus rarely attached dates to his predictions, it is impossible to compile an authentic reproduction of his prophecies for any one year. This French almanac of 1847 was possibly a fake, but used the famous name of Nostradamus.

Left: The Tomb of Nostradamus by Dario Poli.

PART TWO

Left: 'The Dying Planet,' by Dario Poli.

THE VISIONS OF NOSTRADAMUS

DOES PROPHECY have anything to add to our already vast store of knowledge in the twentieth century? Or is it simply the random outpourings of individuals who record and make public their perceived insight into future events? Prediction is still

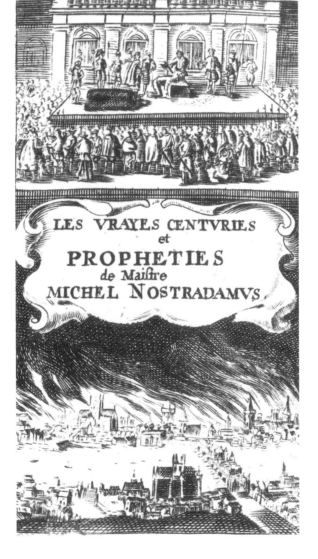

Left: Title page of a seventeenth century edition of the *Centuries* illustrating Nostradamus's predictions of the Great Fire of London and the execution of King Charles I of England.

hugely popular. Alongside crystal-ball-gazing, reading the tea leaves, the Tarot and other ways to glimpse a personal future, are horse-racing tips, weather and Stock Exchange forecasts, and computer predictions in all realms of human activity. The most sophisticated forms of gambling are based on predictive systems, which suggests that even the concept of 'luck' is linked to a belief that the throw of a die or turn of a wheel can be foretold.

Most of this yearning to know about the future stems from a desire for certainty in uncertain times: it is better to know the worst than live in ignorance. As long as humans are driven to seek patterns of cause and effect to explain their often chaotic existence, there will be a place for those who can see beyond the present time.

Pure prophecy – rather than popular prediction – is a time-honoured way of learning about the future through utterances inspired by a divine or supernatural power and viewed by succeeding generations as a vehicle for truthful revelation. Ancient astrology, which involved intuition and meditation linked to the direct observation of the stars and planets in their galaxies, formed a bridge between the old divinatory techniques and pure prophecy.

Nostradamus clearly saw himself as a pure prophet, someone whose predictions should be read and acted upon before it was too late. In the only wholly Latin quatrain in the *Centuries*, which he calls 'Invocation of the law against inept critics', he warns:

Qui legent hos versus, mature censunto;
Prophanum vulgus & inscium ne attrectato.
Omnesque Astrologi, Blenni, Barbari Procul
 sunto,
Qui aliter faxit, is rite sacer esto.
CVI Q100

Let those who read these verses reflect deeply
 upon them,
Let those who have a contempt for sacred things
 and those who shun learning keep their
 distance,
Let astrologers, fools and the ignorant avoid my
 verses,
Whoever does otherwise, a curse shall fall upon
 them.

The predictions chosen for inclusion in this book are a mix of provable 'direct hits' and visions of the not-too-distant future. Nostradamus devoted a great many quatrains to the years immediately before and after the millennium. Among the problems he saw humankind as facing at this time are famine, disease, economic collapse and natural disasters. Of equal importance is the coming of the third Antichrist (after Napoleon and Hitler). He will arrive at the end of the century from the East and wage a long and terrible war against three major adversaries. Recent upheavals in the former Eastern bloc, an uneasy Arab-Israeli peace settlement and the emergence of aggressive Third World powers all point to the fact that Nostradamus may be right in this respect too. But are we impotent in the face of these potential calamities?

If prophecy is taken as an irreversible plan of the future, against which we have no free will, we become the hapless victims of our own mistakes and errors of judgement. If, however,

prophecy is viewed as a means of describing probable patterns of events, changes in human behaviour could alter those patterns and inevitable doom may be avoided.

Perhaps the real message of Nostradamus is that the future lies not in our stars but in ourselves and that the salvation of the human race and of the whole planet is in our own hands.

Above: A fanciful interpretation of Nostradamus the astrologer, as conceived by a nineteenth century artist.

GUY FAWKES AND THE GUNPOWDER PLOT

T HE THRONES OF ENGLAND and Scotland were united in 1603 by the accession of James I (VI of Scotland) to the English throne. James had been brought up as a Presbyterian (Scottish Protestant) and continued the pro-Protestant religious policy of his predecessor Elizabeth.

Nostradamus, a firm believer in the sanctity of the monarchy, sees that a band of conspirators in London will one day attempt to assassinate their king.

Trente de Londres secret conjureront,
Contre leur Roi sur le pont entreprinse,
Lui, satalites la mort degousteront.
Un Roi asleu blonde, natif de Frize.
CIV Q89

Thirty Londoners will secretly conspire,
Against their King, the plot shall be made upon
*   the bridge,*
The court will taste death,
A fair King will be elected, born in the
*   Netherlands.*

Left: The conspirators of the Gunpowder Plot including Guy Fawkes and the leader of the group, Robert Catesby. Fawkes was taken into the conspiracy when it was decided that a man with military expertise was needed to carry out the operation.

Guy Fawkes served in the Spanish army in the Netherlands from 1593 to 1604. He returned to England at the invitation of Robert Catesby, the instigator of the Gunpowder Plot.

Fawkes, Catesby and their fellow conspirators – the increase in numbers to thirty contributed to the eventual discovery of the plot – were unhappy with the increasing oppression of Roman Catholics in England (Fawkes himself, though born to Protestant parents, had converted to Catholicism at an early age). When England and Spain reached a peace agreement in 1604, the Catholics felt that their last chance of help from abroad had slipped away. Their plan was to blow up the Palace of Westminster while James I, his Queen and eldest son met with government ministers inside. Fawkes rented a cellar that extended under the building and planted at least twenty barrels of gunpowder there, camouflaged with coals and bundles of wood.

The plot was discovered when one of the conspirators, Francis Tresham, warned his brother-in-law, Lord Monteagle, not to attend Parliament. He, in turn, warned the King. Fawkes was caught red-handed, tortured, tried and found guilty before a special commission and executed in sight of the Parliament building in 1606. (Catesby was killed while resisting arrest.) In January 1606 Parliament established 5th November as a day of public thanksgiving.

The final two lines of the quatrain refer to the latter part of the seventeenth century. Increasingly dissatisfied with King James II's pro-Catholic policies and concerned when James's Catholic wife produced a male heir to the throne, the Protestant opposition 'invited' the invasion of the fair-haired Prince William of Orange, who was married to James's daughter, Mary. In what became known as the 'Glorious Revolution', James fled the country and, in 1689, the throne passed to William and Mary, who are regarded as the first British constitutional monarchs.

Above: The bodies of the conspirators are hanged, drawn and quartered in the streets of London. Only after he had been severely tortured on the rack did Guy Fawkes reveal the names of his accomplices. They were tried and found guilty of treason before a special commission on 27th January 1606.

THE ENGLISH CIVIL WAR

ALTHOUGH NOSTRADAMUS did not, in general, focus on political events outside France, he undoubtedly made some clear predictions for the turbulent period of English history which included the Civil War of 1642–49, the execution of the hereditary king, Charles I (believed by Royalists – and Nostradamus, a convinced monarchist – to rule by divine right) and the accession of Oliver Cromwell, a skilful Parliamentarian who was able to win the confidence and support of the army.

The mid-seventeenth century was a time of religious divisions in England and Scotland. The Puritan movement was so strong in London that it won a majority in the House of Commons. One of the major problems between Charles and his Parliament stemmed from his marriage to Henrietta Maria of France (a Catholic) in 1625. On his wedding day Charles decreed that all persecution of Catholics must cease. The Puritans were outraged. Increased conflict between their Parliamentarian supporters and Charles's Royalist followers was inevitable and led to the outbreak of hostilities in 1642.

Nostradamus's severe disapproval of any attack on a hereditary monarch gives rise to a scathing criticism of Oliver Cromwell.

Plus Macelin que roi en Angleterre
Lieu obscure nay par force aura l'empire
Lasche sans foi, sans loi saignera terre,
Son temps approche si presque je soupire.
CVIII Q76

More of a butcher than a king in England,
Born of obscure rank will gain Empire by force.
Coward without faith, without law he will bleed
*   the land;*
His time approaches so close that I sigh.

Cromwell refused the throne of England, but he nevertheless ruled like a king, earning the condemnation of Nostradamus for the terrible bloodshed of the Civil War. Cromwell was indeed of obscure rank. Born a commoner, he

Below: King Charles I at a cockfight, in more peaceful times prior to the outbreak of the Civil War. Seventeenth century Dutch School.

Left: Oliver Cromwell, as second in command to the Parliamentary forces, leads the charge at the Battle of Marston Moor in 1644 in this picture by Abraham Cooper.

Below: The death of King Charles I, from a seventeenth century edition of the *Centuries.* Charles surrendered to the Roundheads in 1646 and was charged with high treason. He refused to recognise the legality of the court at his trial stating that 'a king cannot be tried by any superior jurisdiction on earth.' His death sentence was read out on 27 January 1649.

led the life of a quiet country squire before his election as an M. P. prompted his entry into the volatile arena of national politics.

In his reference to Cromwell's lack of faith (that is, the 'true' Roman Catholic faith), Nostradamus draws attention to Cromwell's Protestantism, another point in his disfavour. In conversational tone he relates how, when he made this prophecy, he sighed at the imminence of the events he predicted. Oliver Cromwell was born only thirty years after Nostradamus's death.

The outcome of the Civil War and seven years of bitter fighting was the defeat and imprisonment of Charles I in 1648.

> *La forteresse aupres de la Tamise*
> *Cherra par lors le Roi dedans serré,*
> *Aupres du pont sera veu en chemise*
> *Un devant mort, puis dans le fort barré.*
> CVIII Q37

> *The fortress near the Thames,*
> *Will fall when the King is imprisoned within,*
> *He will be seen near the bridge in his shirt,*
> *One facing death, then locked inside the*
> *fortress.*

At Preston, Parliamentary forces defeated the Scots, with whom Charles was negotiating in secret, effectively ending the Civil War. On 23rd December 1648 Charles I was taken down the river Thames and imprisoned in Windsor

Above: After rejecting the title of King, Oliver Cromwell ruled as 'Lord Protector' of England, Scotland and Ireland between 1653 and 1658. Under his puritanical leadership, dancing, horse-racing and Sunday sports were all forbidden.

Castle, which had fallen to the Parliamentarians. A month or so later, his trial over and in the bitter cold of 30th January 1649, Charles was returned to London and led to a scaffold erected outside Inigo Jones's Banqueting Hall in Whitehall. To prevent him from shivering, and thereby giving an impression of fear, Charles asked for two shirts.

The scene of the execution was crowded with spectators, one of whom was the schoolboy Samuel Pepys who wrote that he would never forget the sound that broke from the crowd as the axe fell. 'Such a groan as I never heard before, and desire I may never hear again.'

The execution of Charles was put into a remarkably accurate European context by Nostradamus in this quatrain.

Gand & Bruceles marcheront contre Envers
Senat du Londres mettront à mort leur Roi
Le sel & vin lui seront à l'envers,
Pour eux avoir le regne en dessarroi.
CIX Q49

Ghent and Brussels march against Antwerp,
The Parliament of London will put their king to
*   death;*
The salt and wine will oppose him,
Because of them he will have the kingdom in
*   trouble.*

In the same year that Charles I was imprisoned, Philip IV of Spain attempted to reconquer the Netherlands. He arrived with his army at Antwerp, which had been a border town of the Spanish possessions since 1579 when Holland (along with several other states) had detached itself from the Low Countries. The third line of this quatrain has intrigued most commentators. The interpretation given by Chas A. Ward is that wisdom and power ('le sel et vin' were common metaphors for these virtues) will – when the forecast events happen – be thrown into their wrong aspects and converted into their opposites, intrigue and violence.

And is it coincidence that this quatrain is numbered 49, the year of King Charles's death?

Nostradamus predicts the repercussions of the execution of Charles I.

> *Du regne Anglois l'indigne dechasse,*
> *Le conseiller par ire mis à feu:*
> *Ses adhera iront si bas tracer,*
> *Que le batard sera demi receux*
> CIII Q80

> *The unworthy man is chased out of the English*
> *   kingdom.*
> *The counsellor through anger will be burnt.*
> *His followers will stoop to such depths*
> *The Pretender will almost be received.*

It is not Charles I who is 'chased out' of his kingdom, but his son, Charles II, who was forced into exile abroad after his defeat by Cromwell in 1651. Burning at the stake was a common method of execution at this time for anyone who opposed the victorious Parliamentarians, and the counsellor may be a reference to Archbishop Laud, architect of Charles I's religious policies, who was burned for treason in 1645. The followers who 'stoop to such depths' of the third line, are the Scots. In 1646 Charles surrendered to the Scots at Newark. They handed him over to Parliament, but he was taken by the army some months later. He escaped to the Isle of Wight and reopened negotiations with the Scots, which precipitated his final downfall. The Pretender who is almost received into the kingdom is Oliver Cromwell, a man who has no natural right to rule but who, nevertheless, as Lord Protector, becomes all but King of England.

Above: The monarchy was re-established in 1660 with the coronation of Charles II, the 'merry monarch'. The years of his reign, known as the Restoration period, brought an end to the English republic. Portait by Wallerant Vaillant.

THE GREAT PLAGUE
AND FIRE OF LONDON

Below: The Great Plague of London 1665-66 killed 70,000 people in a population of 460,000 At its height in September 1665, over a thousand corpses a day were being buried in communal graves.

A CONFIRMED monarchist, Nostradamus viewed the execution of Charles I in 1649 with horror and outrage. His belief in the sanctity of kingship was so strong that he saw this act as a crime worthy of divine retribution.

Nostradamus predicts the Great Plague as punishment for regicide.

La grande peste de cité maritime,
Ne cessera que mort ne soit vengée
Du juste sang par pris damné sans crime,
De la grand dame par feincte n'outragée.
CII Q53

The great plague of the maritime city,
Will not cease until death is avenged,
By just blood taken and condemned for no crime,
The great lady is outraged by the deception.

The 'maritime city' is a description frequently used of London where plague broke out in 1665. It has been suggested that the great lady who is outraged is the Roman Catholic Church which, from Nostradamus's viewpoint, would have strongly opposed the re-establishment of Protestantism less than twenty-five years later under King William III. The 'just blood' probably refers to innocent ('just') Londoners, stricken with the plague although they supported the Royalist cause: tens of thousands died of the disease. (Or is Nostradamus referring to Charles's 'just' blood?) The prediction in the second line suggests that the plague will last as long as it takes to avenge Charles's death. In fact, it lasted about a year.

The avenging plague of 1665 was the last outbreak of the disease in London. The great fire, which followed one year later, helped to prevent its recurrence by destroying many of the crowded streets and alleyways in which carrier rats thrive.

Le sang de juste à Londres fera faulte,
Brusles par fouldres de vingt trois les six:
La dame antique cherra de place haute,
Des mesme secte plusieurs seront occis.
CII Q51

The blood of the just will be dried up in
London,
Burned by fire in three times twenty and six,
The ancient lady will fall from her high
position,
Many of the same denomination will be killed.

This quatrain is interesting because it is one of the few in which Nostradamus attempts an accurate dating which can be checked with historical events. The ancient lady is the statue of the Virgin from St Paul's, which was destroyed in the fire. Other Catholic churches (that is, of the same denomination) were also destroyed (around eighty parish churches in all were burned, along with perhaps 13,000 homes), together with those who sheltered from the flames inside their stone walls (the fierce heat tore through stone, as well as wooden, buildings). Other victims, innocent Royalists, were consumed in the conflagration – a fact lamented, but seen as inevitable, by Nostradamus.

Above: The Great Fire of London,1666, was the worst in the city's long history. It raged for four days and destroyed most of the city, including many civic buildings and 87 parish churches. A fifth of the population lost their homes.

THE BRITISH EMPIRE

'Nothing in the early existence of Britain indicated the greatness she was destined to obtain.'
Thomas Macaulay

AT THE TIME Nostradamus was writing about the British Empire it had neither the political nor the military might of other European countries such as Spain, France or the Holy Roman Empire. The country was in turmoil. Henry VIII had broken England's ties with Rome, a policy continued during the reign of his son Edward VI (1547–53). On her accession, however, Mary had attempted to return the country to Catholicism. Her heir and half-sister, Elizabeth, daughter of Henry VIII and Anne Boleyn, was a Protestant.

Not only does Nostradamus see England's future as a great empire, he also sees how England will defend her worldwide colonies with military might.

Le grand empire sera par Angleterre,
Le pompotam des ans plus de trois cens:
Grandes copies passer par mer & terre,
Les Lusitains n'en seront pas contens.
CX Q100

Right: A superb illustrated child's map of the British Empire, 1886, displays the extent of British territorial gains and the diverse range of races and cultures which fell under her rule.

There will be a great empire in England,
The most powerful force for more than three
hundred years,
Great armies will travel by land and sea,
The Portuguese will not be happy.

Nostradamus predicts that the British Empire will last for three hundred years, which is usually taken as beginning with the reign of Elizabeth I (who ascended the throne in 1558) and ending with the death of Queen Victoria in 1901. Elizabeth's reign was one of exploration. Francis Drake annexed the coast of California for his queen and Humphrey Gilbert claimed Newfoundland. Walter Raleigh (Gilbert's half-brother) reached and attempted – unsuccessfully – to found a colony in an area of North America he called Virginia in Elizabeth's honour (the land corresponds to present-day North Carolina). He also introduced the potato and tobacco to England. More widespread and permanent settlement of these new territories followed in the seventeenth century with the establishment of companies to promote permanent trading links between the mother country and its new colonies.

In the eighteenth century Britain lost its American colonies, but retained control over Canada and India, and established colonies in Africa and Australia. The aftermath of the Napoleonic wars brought territorial gains in

the West Indies. Consolidation and expansion in the nineteenth century were phenomenal, particularly during Victoria's sixty-four year reign. At its height, the British Empire was said to be one on which the sun never set.

One reason for British success in empire building was the early realization that attempted expansion on the neighbouring continent of Europe would be doomed to failure. That, together with the development of its sea power, made the British empire at its zenith unassailable.

The reference to the Portuguese suggests that, as the first great seafaring nation in Europe and empire builders themselves with territories in Africa and South America, they were less than happy about this new and expansionist naval power.

Left: Victoria, Queen of Great Britain (1819-1901) on her Diamond Jubilee. During her long reign, Britain's imperial power reached its height; the country controlled almost one quarter of the world's population.

Left: Captain James Cook was one of the greatest navigators in history. He added Australia and New Zealand to the British Empire and charted most of the Pacific. His voyages on board the *Endeavour* created new standards in cartography, navigation and seamanship.

Left: In 1569 Walter Raleigh fought for the French Hugenots during the French Wars of Religion and later studied Law before becoming an explorer. He set up the English colony in Virginia, naming it after Elizabeth I, the 'virgin' queen.

THE FRENCH
REVOLUTION

A RECURRENT THEME of the *Centuries*, and one which seems to preoccupy Nostradamus, is the period of the first French republic and the Napoleonic empire which followed it. There is no concentration of quatrains devoted to this particular time; they are scattered throughout the ten books of the *Centuries* with no regard for chronology or other structured grouping. Some predict with great accuracy events which were to occur more than two hundred years later. Nostradamus saw clearly the upheaval that would take place when the common man finally took a stand against the power, privilege and corruption of the *ancien régime*.

The French Revolution lasted ten violent and bloody years and transformed France from an absolute monarchy into a modern nation with political power transferred to the middle classes. The revolutionaries were not initially against the concept of monarchy, but Louis XVI's refusal to co-operate with their demands for change forced the revolutionaries to take steps to remove him.

The following two quatrains are remarkable for the accuracy of detail with which they refer to the flight of Louis XVI and Marie Antoinette from Paris in 1791 to the obscure location of Varennes.

De nuict viendra par la forest de Reines,
Deux pars vaultort Herne la pierre blanche,
La maine noir en gris dedans Varennes
Esleu cap. cause tempeste feu sang tranche.
CIX Q20

By night will come through the forest of Reins
A married couple by a roundabout way, the
* queen, the white stone,*
The monk king dressed in grey at Varennes
The elected Capet causes tempest, fire and
* bloody slicing.*

By 1791 Louis XVI felt that the tide of revolutionary feeling against him was so strong that he must flee Paris. His unpopular wife, Marie Antoinette, insisted that she and their children should not be left alone. On 21st June, the whole family, Marie Antoinette dressed grandly in white and Louis in grey posing as her valet, left

the Tuileries Palace through a door in the Queen's apartments. Incompetent preparations – the liveried grooms were viewed with suspicion and did not know their way through Paris – and several delays made the party highly conspicuous. The large carriage, drawn by six horses and normally reserved for royalty, inevitably attracted attention. Their route was to take them through the forest of Reins, but they lost their way and found themselves taking a roundabout way ('*vaultort*').

It is probable that the white stone in the third line refers to the infamous 'affair of the diamond necklace' which involved Marie Antoinette (who wanted a tremendously expensive diamond necklace but could not ask Louis to pay for it), a credulous cardinal (who guaranteed the necklace's worth to the banker who owned it against the promise of a return to the Queen's favour) and Cagliostro (an Italian adventurer who dealt in magic, who was made scapegoat for the affair when it came to Louis's attention). The affair had finally ruined the reputation of the unpopular Queen.

Louis is referred to as an elected or chosen Capet, a name not strictly applicable to the Royal House of Bourbon, but used here in the loose sense of reigning monarch. (The House of Capet had ruled France from 987 to 1328.) The last line suggests that the king, who was the cause of the revolution, was also one of its victims: Louis XVI and Marie Antoinette went to the guillotine, an execution graphically described as 'bloody slicing'.

Nostradamus predicts the arrest of Louis XVI and Marie Antoinette.

Le part solus mari sera mitré,
Retour conflict passera sur le thuille:
Par cinq cens un trahir sera tiltré,
Narbon & Saulce par conteuax avons d'huile.
CIX Q34

Left: Louis bade farewell to his family in the temple on 20th January 1793. Formerly the meeting house of the Knight's Templar, the temple became the state prison during the Revolution and the royal family were taken there in August 1793. Louis's execution took place the following day.

The partner, solitary but married, will be mitred,
The return, worn by fighting he will pass through the Tuileries.
By five hundred one traitor will be ennobled.
Narbonne and Saulce, we will have oil for knives.

This quatrain is extraordinary for its specific and unambiguous detail. Louis and Marie

Antoinette were apprehended at Varennes by a *procureur* named Saulce, whose family (modern spelling Sauce) had been spice merchants and chandlers in the town since the sixteenth century. One of his key activities was the sale of oil. The fact that the King alone is 'mitred' refers to events following the couple's arrest and return to the Tuileries. As the political situation worsened, it became increasingly clear to the revolutionaries that Louis would not accept the constitutional monarchy that they proposed. On 10th August 1792, a Paris mob, reportedly of 500, stormed the Tuileries, forcing on Louis the indignity of wearing the red cap of liberty, a headpiece which is shaped like a bishop's mitre. From this point on, the fate of the royal couple was sealed.

The Comte de Narbonne was the King's war minister, replaced by a 'traitor' from among the revolutionaries.

Napoleon's coming to power was an unwelcome event for Nostradamus. Bonaparte was *'d'un nom farouche'*, of a barbaric name (CI Q76) and *'D'un nom qui onques ne fut au Roy Gallois'*, of a name which was never borne by a French king (CIV Q54). The prophet viewed Napoleon as a 'fearful thunderbolt' who would not only usurp the line of French kings but would make Italy, Spain and the English tremble (CIV Q54). He was also the first of the three Antichrists whose arrivals Nostradamus predicted.

Nostradamus makes clear his poor opinion of Napoleon Bonaparte.

Un empereur naistra pres d'Italie
Qui a l'Empire sera vendu bien cher:
Diront avec quels gens il se ralie,
Qu'on trouvera moins prince que bouche.
CI Q60

An Emperor will be born near Italy,
Who will cost the Empire very dearly.
They will say with what people he keeps
*   company,*
He will be found less a prince than a butcher.

Napoleon Bonaparte was born on the French island of Corsica, which is indeed 'near Italy'. Nostradamus describes the French empire, which he foresaw, as paying a very high price in manpower and political strength for Napoleon's military ambitions. Although the death toll in his campaigns ran into hundreds of thousands, it can be argued that the administrative, educational, legal and military reforms he introduced created for France a more glorious reputation than she has enjoyed before or since.

Nostradamus, the confirmed royalist, would not have seen it that way at all. Those

Above: The Battle of Aboukir, Egypt, by Louis Francois Lejeune. On 25 July 1799, Napleon's expeditionary troops almost completely anihilated the Turkish army of some 18,000 men, during a confrontation on the Nile delta.

who supported Napoleon and his armies and those with whom he kept company were French revolutionaries whose republican ideals Nostradamus deplored. By joining forces with them to guard against the return of the established monarchy, Napoleon forsook the virtues of a prince and espoused those of a butcher.

If there is any doubt as to the identity of the subject of Nostradamus's visions, in its mixture of word play and anagrams, CVIII Q1 makes it very clear.

PAU, NAY, LORON plus feu qu'à sang sera.
Laude nager, fuir grand au surrez.
Les agassas entree refusera.
Pampon, Durance les tiendra enferrez.
CVIII Q1

Pau, Nay Loron will be more fire than blood
In praise to swim, the great one will swim to
    the confluence [of rivers]
He will refuse entry to the magpies
Pampon and the Durance will keep them
    confined.

Nostradamus is here indulging his love of anagrams: Pau, Nay, Loron becomes 'Napaulon Roy', the Corsican spelling of Napoleon Roi, Napoleon the king. He also indulges his love of word play. *Agassas*, is Provençal for 'magpie', which in French is *pie* . Pie is also the French for Pius, and refers to Pius VI or VII who were both imprisoned by Napoleon, Pius VI in 1798 after

Napoleon had marched into Rome, and his successor in 1809 when the Papal States were formally annexed by France and Pius was taken to France to sanction the annexation. The confluence of the rivers is a reference to Valence where the Rhône and Isère flow into one another and where Pope Pius VI was taken to die in 1799.

Below: Napoleon wished to be crowned emperor by Pope Pius VII, to make his ceremony even more impressive than that of any French king. At the last moment, Napoleon took the crown from the Pope's hands and set it on his head himself.

THE DISCOVERIES OF LOUIS PASTEUR

IN THE SIXTEENTH century the causes of many diseases, and the means by which infections were transmitted, were matters of speculation. Since doctors had to rely on a small body of scientific knowledge, medical treatments that worked were often a matter of luck: extraordinary cures were prescribed and taken, and if they happened to be successful, it was probably a coincidence. There were also, of course, herbal and other remedies, which had been handed down through the centuries, and while some of these defy medical and scientific analysis today, it is important to remember that even contemporary medicine does not have all the answers.

Nostradamus not only appears to have based his medical practices on scientific infor-mation that was as yet undiscovered, but his predictions also show that he had specific knowledge of momentous advances in the field of medicine.

The revolutionary discovery by Louis Pasteur that microorganisms which cause souring or decay in food could be destroyed without tainting the food is predicted by Nostradamus in the following quatrain.

Perdu trouvé, caché de si long siecle,
Sera Pasteur demi Dieu honoré:
Ains que la lune acheve son grand siecle
Par autre vents sera deshonoré.
CI Q25

The lost thing is discovered, hidden for many
  centuries.
Pasteur will be celebrated almost as a godlike
  figure.
This is when the moon completes her great
  cycle,
But by other rumours he shall be dishonoured.

The discovery that microorganisms caused a multitude of infections and illnesses was one of the most important in medical history. This knowledge, which is so vital to our daily health and which was 'hidden for many centuries', was not acquired until the late nineteenth century. French chemist Louis Pasteur studied

Below: In 1860, Louis Pasteur, shown here at work in his laboratory, developed the process known as 'pasteurization', a means of heating milk and beer to kill harmful bacteria without affecting the taste.

the process of fermentation, noting that fermentation only occurred when certain microorganisms were present. If these microorganisms are absent, or excluded, beer, wine and vinegar are not tainted and milk does not sour. The corollary holds good in other spheres: the microorganisms that cause putrefaction in a skin wound, though present in the atmosphere all the time, cannot enter a wound if they are excluded from the place where that wound occurs. (Joseph Lister was able to build on this knowledge in his work on sterilization and it is the foundation of all operating-theatre practices today.) Pasteur discovered that the microorganisms that cause milk to sour could be removed by heating the milk. This process, which does not affect the taste of the milk, was named after him and pasteurization is still in use in the milk and cheese industries today.

Pasteur's later discoveries had equally far-reaching effects. He realized that by taking and isolating the microorganism that causes a disease it is possible to produce a strain that can be used to make animals or people immune to that disease. His first success was with chicken

cholera, followed by anthrax and then rabies. He also successfully produced a vaccine against cholera in children.

Acclaimed by the *Encyclopaedia Britannica* as a *'demi-Dieu* [immortal in English versions] ... the acknowledged head of the greatest chemical movement of the time', Pasteur inaugurated the Institute Pasteur in Paris on 14th November 1888 primarily to treat humans suffering from rabies. Nostradamus's sympathies with Pasteur's struggles against some of the authorities of his day are clear from the last line of the quatrain. Pasteur frequently had to defend his ideas and discoveries against hostile opposition. He did so through hard work, experiment and observation.

Left: Louis Pasteur examining fermentation in wine, by Callot. Pasteur became the dean of a new science faculty at the University of Lille in 1854 where his studies into fermentation began.

Below: Nostradamus foresaw the difficulties Pasteur's work would face. In its early years, vaccination was met with fear and hysteria by the general public, as this illustration from a publication of the Anti-Vaccine Society clearly demonstrates.

THE RISE AND FALL OF MUSSOLINI

THE CHANGES BROUGHT ABOUT by the First World War and the spread of communism in eastern Europe caused a reaction in Italy, and elsewhere, the result of which was a new ideological movement. Its founder was Benito Mussolini and its name – derived from the *fasces*, an ancient Roman symbol of authority consisting of a bundle of rods and an axe – was fascism.

Born in 1883, Mussolini, the son of a blacksmith, espoused his father's left-wing principles and integrated them with ideas which he drew from extensive reading of modern philosophers, such as the German Friedrich

Nietzsche. From an early age he was convinced that a great destiny was in store for him. While still a boy, he told his mother 'One day I will make the earth tremble'.

He became editor of the Socialist newspaper *Avanti!* in 1904, but was forced to resign and was expelled from the Party in 1914 for refusing to support Italy's neutrality in the First World War (he called for Italy to fight on the side of the Allies and was himself wounded while serving at the front). He founded his own newspaper, *Il Popolo d'Italia,* which increasingly became a platform for his fascist views. In 1919 he founded the fascist movement whose blackshirt squads were employed against local socialists, communists, Catholics and liberals. In October 1921, profiting from the economic and political instability in postwar Italy, he converted the movement into the Fascist Party, which won control of a number of provincial cities. In 1922 the Blackshirts organized a show of strength, marching on Rome and entering the city unopposed by government or army. In October, faced with the man who saw himself as the only hope of preventing the country slipping into further turmoil, King Victor Emmanuel III gave Mussolini leave to form a coalition government. By 1929, he had imposed

a single-party dictatorship, giving himself the title of *Il Duce,* the Leader.

His initial social policies, programme of public works and law and order campaigns were popular, but his increasingly aggressive foreign policy was ill considered.

Nostradamus foresees many of the interesting details of Mussolini's career and predicts his humiliating end.

Le grand naistra de Veronne & Vincence,
Qui portera un surnon bien indigne.
Qui a Venise vouldra faire vengeance.
Lui mesmeprins homme du guet & signe.
CVIII Q33

The great one of Verona and Vincenza,
Who bears a very unworthy name,
Who will want to take vengeance at Venice,
Himself seized by a vigilante.

The subject of this quatrain is clear from the second line: Benito Mussolini's surname literally means 'muslin maker', considered to be a humble (unworthy) profession. Mussolini's troops invaded Abyssinia (Ethiopia) in 1935, in response to which Britain and the League of

Left: The Italian advance on Abyssinia in October 1935. Despite the tremendous size of Abyssinia and the extreme hostility of the terrain, the Italian army's enthusiasm for this campaign and its rapid victory, made this one of the fastest conquests in modern military history.

Right: The dead bodies of Mussolini and his lover, Claretta Petacci hang from the burnt-out shell of a Milan petrol station, 1945.

Nations imposed economic sanctions on Italy, frustrating Mussolini's dream of a new Roman empire, *Mare Nostrum*. Hitler saw an opportunity to secure a military and economic alliance with Italy in order to strengthen his ties with another fascist state and continued to supply Italy with raw materials despite the sanctions. This resulted in Mussolini giving the Germans his support in 1940 when Hitler's armies seemed invincible. Disastrous military reversals for the Italians in Russia, Greece and North Africa, together with food shortages and low morale, caused a growing dependence on Hitler's support and this, in conjunction with the increasing likelihood of an allied victory, led his party to arrest him on 25th July 1943. He was liberated by German paratroopers and set up by Hitler as the puppet ruler of the newly formed republic of Saló in German-occupied northern Italy from where he continued to dream of restoring Italy to fascism.

In the last line Nostradamus foresees the capture of Mussolini and his mistress, Claretta Petacci, by a partisan leader (vigilante) in April 1945 on the shores of Lake Como as they were attempting to leave Italy.

In the words of Luigi Barzini, author of *The Italians*: 'They were both shot against the ornate gate of a pompous villa the next morning. The woman had tried to shield his body and was mown down with him. The money and documents [Mussolini was reputed to be carrying sums of money and documents that he hoped would clear him should he be tried as a war criminal] disappeared for ever. The bodies were taken to Milan and hung feet high, from a petrol station roof, alongside those of all other Fascist chiefs caught and killed on the same road, on their way to Switzerland. '

Perhaps Mussolini should be allowed to have the last word on this interesting prediction. Thirteen years before his death, he had told a colleague: 'Everybody dies the death that corresponds to his character.' The people he had deluded had found a way to pay him back.

FRANCO AND THE SPANISH CIVIL WAR

SPAIN MAINTAINED her neutrality during the First World War, in the aftermath of which Primo de Rivera established a military dictatorship which undermined the position of the monarchy. Rivera was deposed in 1930 and the king abdicated a year later when a republic was proclaimed. The victory of the Popular Front (a coalition of the Republican left, the communists and the socialists, which represented all the major working-class interests) in February 1936 was the prelude to civil war. It is evident from a number of the quatrains that Nostradamus foresaw the turmoil which was to take place in Spain during the 1930s and 1940s, and the devastating schism of civil war.

Nostradamus clearly names two of the principal protagonists in the troubled period of the Civil War – Francisco Franco and Juan Antonio Primo de Rivera.

De Castel Franco sortira l'assemblee,
L'ambassadeur non plaisant fera scisme;
Ceux de Riviere seront en la meslee,
Et au grand goulphre desnier ont l'entree.
CIX Q16

From Castile Franco will drive out the assembly,
The ambassadors will not agree and cause a schism.
Followers of Riviera will be in the crowd,
And the great man will be denied entry into the gulf.

In 1926, at the age of thirty-four, Francisco Franco became Europe's youngest general. He was appointed chief of the General Staff in 1935. Forces hostile to the Popular Front government (grouped together as the Nationalists and including monarchists, Catholics and Spanish fascists – the Falange) staged a rebellion. Franco joined the Nationalists, flying to Morocco and taking over the Spanish garrison there, then advanced with his troops into southern Spain. By October 1936 he was head of state in the Nationalist zone. (Juan Antonio Primo de Rivera, founder of the Falange and

Left: A propaganda poster issued by the Marxist movement, P.O.U.M., during the civil war reads, 'Peasants the Land is Yours'.

son of the former dictator, was imprisoned and executed by the Popular Front government when war broke out.)

The first line of this quatrain refers to Franco's invasion of Spain when he tried to drive out the existing Republican national assembly in Madrid. The result was the 'schism' of civil war between Franco's Nationalist forces and the Republicans. There are various interpretations of the last line of the quatrain. Although ideologically close to Italy and Germany, Franco kept Spain neutral during the Second World War (probably because Hitler was not prepared to cede France's territories in north Africa to Franco, the price of the Spaniard's support). The Axis powers were, therefore, denied access through the Strait of Gibraltar to the 'gulf' of the Mediterranean.

Civil War is foreseen as a great wound from which the country and her people will bleed.

L'un des plus grands fuira aux Espaignes
Qu'en longue playe apres viendra saigner:
Passant copies par les hautes montaignes
Devastant tout & pius en paix regner.
CIII Q54

Right: The sight of buildings shattered by massive air raids and streets blocked by debris met the Nationalist Army as they made their final advance on Spain's capital, Madrid, in November 1936.

One of the great men will flee into Spain
Which will then bleed from a great wound
Troops will pass over high mountains
destroying everything
And afterward he shall reign in peace.

Here Nostradamus speaks of the 'great wound' from which Spain will 'bleed'. The Spanish Civil War, which lasted for three years (1936–39), involved fierce fighting and blood-shed, much of which took place in high mountain areas. Some 700,000 Spaniards died.

To complete his prediction, Nostradamus forecasts that there will be a period of peace in Spain ('afterward he shall reign in peace'). To confirm the country's neutrality during the Second World War, in 1955 Spain joined the United Nations and in 1956 withdrew from northern Morocco. Franco's modernization of the Spanish economy in the 1950s and 1960s paved the way for the dismantling of the total-itarian regime which he had established. On his death in 1975 Nostradamus's prophecy was fulfilled – the Generalissimo had ruled in peace for thirty-six years. His chosen successor, King Juan Carlos, completed the country's transition to democracy.

Above: Franco's Nationalist troops arrive at Col de Portus, a pass high in the Pyrenees which Hannibal is also said to have traversed on his long march to Italy about 218 BC.

Right: General Franco is seen here with Don Juan and Juan Carlos of Spain in 1975. Before he died, Franco announced Prince Juan Carlos, the eldest son of the pretender to the Spanish throne, his official successor.

Above: Der Fuhrer gives his infamous Nazi salute to party members. Regarded by many as the second antichrist predicted by Nostradamus, Hitler was responsible for instigating the bloodiest war in history, which caused the deaths of 45 million people.

THE SECOND WORLD WAR

A NUMBER OF Nostradamus's prophecies are concerned with the Second World War of 1939–45 and, particularly, with the man regarded as one of the blackest figures in modern history. Responsible for the deaths of some 3.5 million of his own troops and 6 million Jews (of a total population of 8 million in the countries he occupied), in addition to troops and civilians from all over Europe and American servicemen and women, Adolf Hitler is generally agreed to be the second of the three Antichrists predicted by Nostradamus.

Despite other interpretations, this quatrain makes it clear that Nostradamus was able to see the name Hitler.

Bestes farouche de faim fleuves tranner,
Plus part du champ encontre Hister sera.
En caige de fer le grand fera treisner,
Quand rien enfant de Germain observera.
CII Q24

Wild beasts in hunger will cross the rivers,
Most of the battlefield will fall to Hitler,
He will cause the great one to be drawn into an
*   iron cage,*
When the child of Germany observes no laws.

Nostradamus, who frequently used anagrams of names, uses Hister as the name of the German who observed no (internationally agreed) laws. Although it has been suggested that the word Hister in the original text could refer to the river Danube (*Ister* in Latin), Hitler himself identified with the predictions, after Joseph Goebbels' wife, who was interested in the occult, alerted her husband to their existence in 1939. From about May 1940 onward, Goebbels, Hitler's minister for propaganda since 1933, had quatrains specially forged. These predicted that Hitler would win the war and were incorporated into the propaganda leaflets dropped by German aircraft all over Europe. In retaliation British Intelligence

Left: Joseph Goebbels and his wife, Magda, were devout supporters of Hitler. In the Berlin bunker on 1st May 1945, when defeat seemed imminent, they took their own lives and those of their six children.

Right: The Germans advance on Russian positions in the Caucasus. Despite signing a non-aggression agreement with Stalin in 1939, Hitler's confidence was so strong after his successful invasion of France that on 22nd June 1941, he launched a full-scale attack on Russia.

Below: Images of war, death and destruction merge into one disturbing illustration of the Holocaust by Dario Poli.

forged anti-German 'Nostradamus' quatrains which Allied pilots dropped over France and Belgium as late as 1943.

The first line of the quatrain must refer to the first two years of the Second World War when the Germans crossed rivers in their advance across Europe. Nostradamus foresaw that, in the initial stages of the war at least, Hitler would enjoy the greatest military successes. The 'iron cage' has been variously interpreted as the bomb-shelter bunker in Berlin where Hitler died or more likely, perhaps, as Hitler's ensnarement of General Gamelin's French forces when, after bypassing the Maginot Line, the Germans drew the French into a cage-like trap. (The Maginot Line was a series of military fortifications designed to thwart a military invasion of France, built after the First World War; since the line did not extend along the Belgian–German border, it was easily outflanked by the invaders.)

Hitler's ambition was to revive the medieval Holy Roman Empire (the First Reich) and create a Greater Germany comprising Austria ('annexed' in 1938), Czechoslovakia and Poland (invaded in 1939) and to the west, France, Belgium and Holland, all of which fell in the spring and early summer of 1940, and Great Britain.

Nostradamus pinpoints the extent of Hitler's territorial ambitions.

Translatera en la grand Germanie,
Brabant & Flandres, Gand, Bruges &
Bolongne,
La traifue fainte, le grand duc d'Armenie,
Assaillira Vienne & la Coloigne.
CV Q94

He will change into the Greater Germany
Brabant and Flanders, Ghent, Bruges and
Boulogne.
The truce feigned, the great Duke of Armenia
will assault Vienna and Cologne.

The Greater Germany in this quatrain is the Third Reich with Hitler occupying town after town as he marched across Europe. The feigned truce probably refers to the non-aggression pact Hitler concluded with the Soviet Union in August 1939. This relieved pressure on the eastern front, and allowed him to concentrate on his enemies to the west. The 'Duke of Armenia' is also a reference to the Soviet Union against whom Hitler launched Operation Barbarossa in 1941. It was not until the end of the war, when the Soviet Union had joined the Allies, that Russian troops under their 'great leader', Josef Stalin, marched into Germany from the east, meeting American forces to the south.

Below: The horror of Belsen was revealed to the world when the British Army liberated the camp in 1945 and confirmed the appalling truth about conditions there. Dead bodies were strewn everywhere and those still struggling to stay alive were suffering from the effects of torture and starvation.

Nostradamus sees the eventual downfall of the Nazi leader.

Les fortresses des assiegés serrés,
Par poudre à feu profondes en abisme:
Les proditeurs seront tous vifs serres
Onc aux sacristes n'advint si piteux scisme.
CIV Q40

The fortress of those under siege
Was sunk into the depths by gunpowder
The traitor will be entombed in it alive,
Never before was there so pitiful a schism
among the Germans.

The last days of Hitler's life were spent in a concrete bunker blasted under the Berlin Chancellery. When the Nazis realized that all was lost, one of their wilder schemes was a pact between Germany and Great Britain to fight the Soviet Union – and this at a time when the Allied forces were on the outskirts of Berlin! In this context the last line of the quatrain has the ring of historical truth. With the Allies approaching and only a small contingent of Hitler Youth to protect him, Hitler married his long-standing mistress, Eva Braun, then poisoned her, his dog Blondi and himself. The bunker did indeed become Hitler's tomb.

Above: Russian soldiers raise their flag over the Reichstag after capturing the building in 1945.

Right: 'The End'. An interpretation of Hitler's last moments in the Berlin bunker on 30th April 1945, by Soviet artists Probiry Krylov, Mikhail Kupryanov and Nikola Sokolov.

THE ATOMIC BOMB

I N 1939 AMERICAN scientists, many of them refugees from the fascist regimes of Europe, took steps to organize a project to exploit a newly discovered fission process for military purposes. In March G. B. Pegram of Columbia University arranged a conference between Enrico Fermi (an Italian-born physicist) and the U. S. Navy Department. Fermi was awarded the 1938 Nobel prize for his work on the bombardment of uranium by thermal neutrons; this was the critical process in splitting an atom of uranium, thereby releasing some of the energy within the atom for use as power or, as the subsequent project was to prove, in a single, con-trolled, timed explosion. President Franklin D. Roosevelt awarded $6,000 to fund a United States research programme, with the purpose of producing an atomic bomb before Adolf Hitler's scientists could do so. The project became the most secret scientific endeavour of the Second World War.

In 1942 Fermi succeeded in producing and controlling a fission chain reaction in Chicago. By 1945 the finances of the project, known from 1942 as the Manhattan Project and by this time based in Los Alamos, New Mexico, had esca-lated to $2,000 million and the Americans had made and tested both uranium and plutonium

Above: Professor Enrico Fermi, the Italian born atomic scientist and Nobel prizewinner, was one of the chief architects of the nuclear age.

bombs. The first atomic weapon was tested on 16th July 1945 at Alamogordo, New Mexico.

Nostradamus predicts the dropping of two huge bombs on Hiroshima and Nagasaki.

Aupres des portes & dedans deux cites
Seront deux fléaux & oncques n'apperceu
un tel:
Faim, dedans peste, de fer hors gens boutés,
Crier secours au grand Dieu immortel.
CII Q6

Near the harbour and in two cities
Will be two scourges, the like of which have
never been seen.
Hunger, plague within, people thrown out by
the sword
Will cry for help from the great immortal God.

The first line of this quatrain accurately identifies Hiroshima and Nagasaki, the two seaports (and therefore centres of military and supply bases and industrial plants) chosen as the targets for the two atomic bombs (*'deux fléaux'*). Nostradamus has no words to describe the horror of the two scourges; he had never seen anything to compare with the aftermath of an atomic explosion. Even the sufferings of the plague, with which he was familiar, could not have prepared him for the sight of casualties of radiation burns and sickness and scenes of horrific destruction. He also sees those who had escaped death – hungry, sick and dispossessed – praying for help and relief in their extreme suffering.

Bombs were dropped by American planes on Hiroshima on 6th August 1945 and Nagasaki on the 9th. Some 130,000 people were killed or injured in Hiroshima, and 75,000 in Nagasaki. Both towns were destroyed.

Below: A dramatic photograph of the first atomic bomb test at Alamogordo, New Mexico on 16th July 1945. Convection currents created by such an explosion suck up dust and other materials into a fireball, creating the familiar mushroom-shaped cloud.

Right: The ruins of Hiroshima, Japan, after the United States of America dropped the atomic bomb on 6th August 1945. The explosion instantly devastated four square miles of the centre of the city, killed 66,000 of its citizens and injured a further 69,000. Untold genetic damage was caused by the effects of radiation.

EXTRATERRESTRIALS LAND ON EARTH

'Of course the flying saucers are real – and they are interplanetary.'
Air Chief Marshall Lord Dowding (head of RAF Fighter Command in the Second World War)

'Something unknown to our understanding is visiting this earth.'
Dr Mitrovan Zverev (former USSR) Santiago, Chile

THE TIME FRAME of the prophecies within the *Centuries* is not entirely clear. Until 1582 the Julian calendar, which had been introduced by Julius Caesar in 46 BC, was in use. Since this contained too many leap years, the calendar was running some ten days behind solar time. Pope Gregory amended the calendar to take account of this discrepancy, but his reforms were not adopted in Britain and other Protestant countries (Britain changed in 1752.). Nostradamus seems to have foreseen this period of controversy, which makes accurate dating of events in the *Centuries* difficult. What can be said is that his prophecies can be taken to refer to any time between the 1550s and the end of the world, perhaps in AD 5000. It is possible, therefore, that Nostradamus foresaw visitors to earth from other planets.

Many commentators agree that in this quatrain Nostradamus could be referring to aliens landing on earth.

De nuict soleil penseront avoir veu,
Quand le porceau demi-homme on verra:
Bruict, chant, bataille, au ciel battre apercu:
Et bestes brutes a parler lon orra.
CI Q64

At night they think they will have seen the sun,
When they see the half pig-man:
They will perceive noise, screams and battles in
  the sky,
And brute beasts shall be heard to speak.

When it is difficult to understand what Nostradamus is trying to say, it is important to remember that he must often have groped for words when presented with visions of the high-technology future. In such cases he frequently resorts to figurative language, which is not always intelligible, to describe as accurately as possible those things with which his eye and brain are unfamiliar.

Nostradamus was accustomed to travel by mule and sometimes by horse and cart; in this quatrain he is trying to make sense of a horrifying battle in the night sky, so bright with the lights of many flying machines that it appears as if the sun is shining. The alien pilots of those machines attract his attention, with their face masks, which probably incorporate breathing apparatus to help them to cope in an alien atmosphere, giving them the appearance of pigs' snouts. The last line of the quatrain indicates the fierceness of the battle. The brute beasts, it is generally suggested, refer to the flying craft of the invaders whose engines make such a terrible noise that it seems to Nostradamus as if they are monsters communicating with each other.

Nostradamus was not the only prophet to

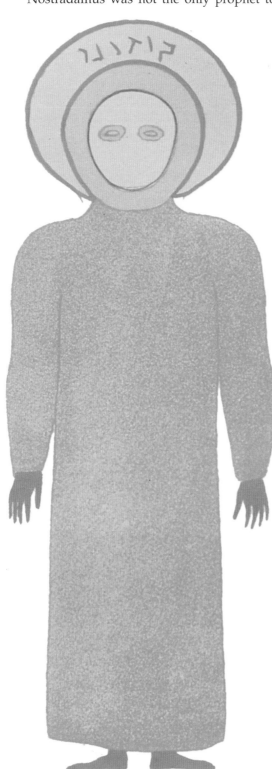

see such visions. Ezekiel also describes terrifying scenes of creatures arriving from the sky. 'I saw a storm wind coming from the north, a vast cloud with flashes of fire and brilliant light about it; and within was a radiance like brass, glowing in the heart of the flames' (Chapter 1). He goes on to describe the vehicles in which these extraordinary creatures made their descent to earth. 'When the living creatures moved, the wheels moved beside them, when the creatures rose from the ground, the wheels rose; they moved in whatever direction the spirit would go; and the wheels rose together with them for the spirit of the living creatures was in the wheels.'

It is probably true to say that people have been watching the skies ever since, although it is particularly in the twentieth century that sky-watching for a flying object that cannot be identified as an aircraft, satellite or known astronomical body has become something of an obsession. The contribution of the mass media

to the debate is undeniable: reports of strange lights in the sky and the unexplained appearances of 'corn circles' are widely disseminated, usually in sensationalist terms. The popular success of the German Erich von Daniken's *Chariots of the Gods?* (in which he proposes that such phenomena as the Nazca lines in Peru, the inscriptions on the carved statues of Easter Island and many prehistoric buildings which are centuries ahead of their time in terms of methods of construction and use of materials, were the work of visitors from other planets) attests to this fascination. So, too, does the popularity of blockbuster movies such as *Close Encounters of the Third Kind*. And, given that men have been in space, landed on the moon, sent cameras to Saturn, Mars and Venus, and have despatched *Voyager* beyond the limits of the solar system, perhaps it is reasonable to suppose that other life forms in the galaxy may be capable of similar technological advances.

At the beginning of the 1990s, the funds of the Search for Extra Terrestrial Intelligence Institute (SETI) in California were doubled and later tripled. Staffed by highly qualified scientists to monitor radio emissions in space for indications of intelligent signals, SETI appears to be taking the subject of finding a signal from an extraterrestrial source very seriously.

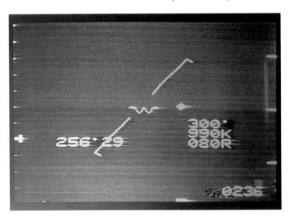

Above: Nazca lines, such as this spider figure, are scattered over the Nazca desert in Peru. Are these giant drawings, some of them thousands of miles in length, pictures of the constellations by which ancient farmers plotted the most propitious time to plant their crops? Or are they runways used by extraterrestrials to make landings on earth?

Left: UFO caught on the radar system of a Belgium F-16 Chaser, 1990. The tracks (white lines) showed such rapid and irregular changes in the object's speed and altitude that they could not possibly have been created by any manmade aircraft.

Above: 'The End of the Papacy'. Crumbling Roman architecture and artefacts are used by Dario Poli to symbolize the eventual disintegration of the papacy and western civilization predicted by Nostradamus.

THE PAPACY

THE MILLENNIUM had a special significance for Nostradamus since it coincides, astrologically, with the move from the Piscean age of his time (an age of unquestioning religious faith and of belief in miracles and magic) into the Aquarian age of probing and reasoning (which astrologer Dr Liz Greene believes will influence organized religion). It is noticeable that many churches and their leaders no longer exert the moral authority they once commanded and that organized religion plays no part in the lives of a great many people.

Many of Nostradamus's prophecies point to the decline of the power of the Papacy. Although his true religious sympathies may have lain elsewhere, Nostradamus would almost certainly have felt that a decline in the influence of the Vatican spelled the end of world order and civilized life as he knew it.

St Malachy, the twelfth-century Irish prelate and prophet appointed Archbishop of Armagh in 1132, shares many of Nostradamus's views on the Papacy. One of Malachy's best-known works was a list of Popes whose characteristics were enshrined in a motto after each name. Thus Benedict XV, who was pontiff during the slaughter of the First World War, was identified by the words *Religio depopulata*, the depopulation of religion. Both Nostradamus and Malachy predicted that there would be only six Popes after Pius XII (who died in 1958), so that only two more will take office after the death of John Paul II. If these prophecies are true, the second millennium may well see the end of the institution of the Papacy.

In 1978 Albino Luciani, Patriarch of Venice, was elected Pope, taking the name John Paul (the names of his two predecessors). Anxious to remove hints of financial impropriety connected with the reign of Pope Paul VI (1963–78), he decided to overhaul the manage-

Below: Pope Benedict XV was elected Pope just one month after the outbreak of the First World War.

ment of the Vatican Bank and started by directing his secretary of state, Cardinal Villot, to begin investigations. He also gave Villot a list of Bank employees whom he suspected of belonging to the P2 masonic lodge and whose members included many international, high-profile politicians, bankers and businessmen. Pope John Paul required that all the men on the list should resign their positions at the Bank or be transferred to another part of the Vatican administration.

Nostradamus foresees that the Cardinals' displeasure will cause them to murder their Pope.

Celui qu'aura gouvert de la grand cappe,
Sera induict à quelques cas patrer
Les douze rouges viendront fouiller la nappe.
Soubz meutre, meutre se viendra perpetrer.
CIV Q11

He who will be covered with a great cloak,
Will be led to carry out certain actions,
The twelve red ones shall soil the table cloth,
Under murder, murder shall be committed.

This quatrain shows Nostradamus's gift for metaphor: the 'twelve red ones' are Cardinals and the 'great cloak' is the Pope. One month after his election (and the day after he had given Villot his 'reshuffle' list), Pope John Paul I died in suspicious circumstances. He had dined with his Cardinals the evening before. His personal staff, who were normally in attendance when he rose, were not there when he was found dead in bed the following morning. Had the Cardinals soiled the tablecloth with poisoned wine?

Nostradamus believes that the Pope will be handed a poisoned chalice.

Below: His Holiness Pope Pius XII gives his blessing to a crowd of more than 200,000 in St Peter's Square. Today, people continue to travel to Rome from all over the world to receive the pope's blessing.

Left: Pope Paul VI, lying in state in St Peter's Cathedral, Rome. On 14th August 1978, many thousands came to pay their last respects and mourn the death of their pontiff.

Below: Pope John Paul I addresses the crowds from the balcony of the Vatican Palace overlooking St Peter's Square, Rome. His pontificate, which lasted just thirty four days, was the shortest in modern history, yet he proved himself to be an extremely popular pope.

Quand le sepulcre du grand Romain trouvé,
Le jour apres sera esleu Pontife:
Du Senat gueres il ne sera prouve,
Empoisonné son sang au sacré scyphe.
CIII Q65

When the tomb of the great Roman shall be
  found,
A Pope will be elected the next day,
Who will not be approved of by the Senate,
Poisoned, his blood in the sacred chalice.

The 'tomb of the great Roman' in the first line of this quatrain could refer to a tomb discovered in Jerusalem in 1978, believed to be that of St Peter. The election of Pope John Paul I occurred in the same year.

There is no proof that John Paul I was murdered – he was reported by Vatican officials to have died of a heart attack, but since no post-mortem examination was carried out there is no way to authenticate that statement – but there are still many unanswered questions surrounding his death.

SEXUAL LICENCE AND THE SPREAD OF AIDS

IT WAS A SIXTEENTH-CENTURY belief that plagues and pestilences were punishments from God. Outbreaks of infectious illnesses caused fear and panic, and sometimes remorse, among the population. Many of today's religious fundamentalists also believe in divine retribution. Nostradamus's writings attest to his belief in a supreme being, the source of all creation, from whom he received prophetic inspiration. He would have looked with sadness at a future when orthodox religion was no longer the guardian of moral values and been deeply disturbed at the decline of sexual standards as a result of the commercial exploitation of sex.

Nostradamus foresees a time of such depravity that pornography will no longer be unlawful.

Pour le plaisir d'edict voluptueux,
On meslera la poison dans l'aloy:
Venus sera en cours si vertueux,
Qu'obfusquera du soleil tout à loi.
CV Q72

For the pleasure of an edict of vice,
Poison shall be mixed with the law,
Venus will be in such great demand,
That it will obscure the brilliance of the sun.

Nostradamus regards the deterioration of moral behaviour that leads to an unbridled pursuit of sex (Venus is the goddess of love) with horror. Could he be hinting in the fourth line that AIDS is a blight on the brightness of sexual love?

Nostradamus predicts the spread of infection and disease, possibly AIDS.

Au port d'Agde trois fustes entreront
Portant d'infect non foi & pestilence
Passant le pont mil milles embleront,
Et le pont rompre à tierce resistance.
CVIII Q21

Three ships will enter the port of Agde,
Carrying with them infection and pestilence,
Passing the bridge they will carry off
*   thousands.*
The bridge is broken by the resistance of the
*   third.*

Opposite page: 'Plague', by Dario Poli. Distorted images of anguish and suffering portray the effects of future viral infections that will sweep through the population in the next millennium.

Left: Gay males kiss in public during a demonstration on behalf of AIDS victims.

Above: An article in the Daily Mirror, from 10th November 1986, highlights public fear and unrest over the devastations of a virus for which there is, as yet, no cure.

The quatrain describes a disease which kills thousands of people, entering Agde – a seaport near Marseilles – by ship. The thousands of victims suggest that the disease could be AIDS carried by passengers and crew from Africa (AIDS is believed to have originated in central Africa, possibly by the mutation of a virus carried by green monkeys).

The spread of AIDS will cause famine and hunger, and it is possible that quarantine areas will be set up for the disease's victims.

Si grand famine par unde pestifere.
Par pluie longue le long du pole arctique,
Samarobrin cent lieux de l'hemishere,
Vivront sans loi exempt de pollitique.
CVI Q5

A very great famine caused by a wave of
*   pestilence,*
Will come as insistently as rain as far as the
*   Arctic pole,*
Samarobrin a hundred leagues from the
*   hemisphere,*
Will live without law; exempt from politics.

Right: Isolation ward for AIDS babies in Romania. The extent of the incidence of this disease among Romanian infants was only uncovered after the fall and execution of President Ceausescu in 1989.

This quatrain has aroused great interest. One interpretation is that a devastating disease will spread to such an extent that it will ultimately reach the Arctic polar regions. The disease has spread from a land where there is great famine and where it is difficult to tell the sick from the starving. (In many parts of Africa AIDS and starvation are already depleting populations.) Nostradamus may have seen an AIDS quarantine hospital or camp named Samarobrin (or an anagram of that name) in the northern hemisphere. The idea is not unrealistic: Fidel Castro has built just such a hospital on Cuba. It requires perhaps only a small leap of the imagination to see such isolation colonies developing into large autonomous communities with their own laws and political structure.

An alternative suggestion is that Samarobrin refers to an unmanned spacecraft which circles the earth at a height of approximately 430 kilometres and which is somehow responsible for the emission of a harmful substance which spreads disease over the northern polar region. (Given the lack of monitoring and control that exist in the realm of experiments in bacteriological and chemical warfare, the idea is not so far-fetched.) It is also worth pointing out that experiments are underway with two drugs which may result in a cure for the disease: 'Suramin' and 'Ribavarin'. Could Nostradamus have simply misunderstood the names, or been indulging in one of his habitual plays on words?

Nostradamus predicts that a sexually transmitted disease will bring shame and ruin to the city of Rome.

O vaste Romone ta ruine s'approche
Non de tes murs de ton sang & substance;
L'aspre par lettres fera si horrible coche
Fer poinctu mis a tous jusques au manche.
CX Q65

Oh great Rome your ruin draws near,
Not of your walls, but of your blood and
  substance,
The sharp by letters, shall make so horrid
  a notch,
Pointed iron thrust in all the way to the shaft.

The invader which will attack Rome and bring about the city's decline will do so by 'blood and substance', destroying its life force but leaving the walls of the buildings undamaged. AIDS is passed through blood and bodily fluids and, as there is no immediate prospect of any cure, is capable of destroying the life force of a city. The 'sharp by letters' refers to the tabloid-press-induced moral backlash against all those practices which are likely to contribute toward the spread of the disease, in particular, casual sex between homosexual males, male and female prostitution (the number of partners increases the risk of sex with someone infected and spreads the virus to subsequent partners) and intravenous drug-taking (sharing a needle with a victim will spread the disease). The infection will degrade and tarnish the reputation ('shall make so horrid a notch') of this once proud city. The choice of Rome as the victim city cannot be accidental: Rome, home of the Catholic Church, is one of the world's greatest historical and artistic centres, founded in the first century BC and the capital of a highly advanced civilization. The last line is a sexual allusion referring to the way AIDS can be transmitted by males (the 'shaft') during sexual intercourse.

Left: Demonstrators quote biblical authority against promiscuity in their campaign against AIDS. 'For if ye live after the flesh, ye shall die: but if ye through Spirit do mortify the deeds of the body, ye shall live.' *Romans 8:13.*

WAR IN THE MIDDLE EAST

THERE ARE MANY references to the East in the *Centuries*. Beyond the influence of Christian power in Europe and dominated by the Moslem infidel, the area referred to today as the Middle East was regarded by Christians in the sixteenth century as the region from which the forces of darkness that would threaten Christendom were most likely to emerge. Indeed, Nostradamus predicts that the third Antichrist will come from the East.

L'Oriental sortira de son siege ...
Et un chacun frappera de sa gaule.
CII Q29

The Oriental one will come from his seat of power ...
And he will strike everyone with his rod.

Equally unequivocal is Nostradamus's prediction that there will be a fearful new dictator in power in Iraq.

Il entrera vilain, mechant, infame
Tyrannisant la Mesopotamie,
Tous amis fait d'adulterine d'ame,
Terre horrible, noir de phisonomie.
CVIII Q70

Right: A propaganda poster from 1988, during the Iran-Iraq War, projects the message of Sadam Hussein as the architect of a prosperous and happy Iraq.

Left: Saddam Hussein's use of chemical weapons on the Kurdish peoples of northern Iraq has literally wiped out entire communities of the population.

He will come, villainous, wicked and infamous,
To tyrannize Mesopotamia,
He makes all friends by an adulterous lady,
The land horrible and blackened.

The 'villanous, wicked and infamous' figure of the first line must surely be Saddam Hussein, president of Iraq since 1979. Prior to his annexation of Kuwait in 1990 in an attempt to expand his control in the Middle East, he had fought an eight-year-long war against Iran and earned worldwide condemnation for his treatment of the Kurdish minority, in particular the chemical attacks on the Kurds' villages in the mountainous northern areas of Iraq. The country is the site of the ancient kingdom of Mesopotamia (literally the land between two rivers, the Tigris and Euphrates), the oldest known civilization in the world.

The reference to the 'adulterous lady' in the third line is not clear at first sight. Indulging his love of deliberate obscurity, however, Nostradamus is perhaps directly comparing the wickedness and corruption of the present dictatorship with the moral turpitude of the Biblical whore of Babylon (Babylon was built on the banks of the Euphrates, south of present-day Baghdad).

The fourth line is an accurate description of the results of the Gulf War. In 1990, under the initiative of Operation Desert Storm, the Western powers attacked Iraq in response to Saddam Hussein's intimidation and invasion of Kuwait. When it became evident that the Western allies were going to win what Saddam

Below: Iraq's military invasion of Kuwait in 1990 instigated the Gulf War. The conflict created massive numbers of refugees who fled to neighbouring countries such as Jordan and Saudi Arabia.

Above: Scene at the battlefront during the Iran-Iraq War, 1986. A United Nations Report later confirmed that during the conflict 50 towns and 4,000 villages were destroyed, 14,000 civilians were killed and 1,250,000 people were displaced.

Below: Smoke blackens the sky from the fires of Kuwaiti oil wells, set alight on the orders of Saddam Hussein. The effect on the environment has been catastrophic.

had called 'the mother of all battles', he set the Kuwaiti oil wells alight. The aftermath of the fires was indeed a 'blackened' land, and an environmental disaster. A pall of smoke darkened the sky and covered the earth for hundreds of kilometres with toxic black residue from the burned oil; and the long-term effects for wildlife in the area may be fatal.

Saddam Hussein continues to terrorize the Kurds in the north of his country and the Shia Moslems in the marshlands to the south. It is widely believed that, contrary to international agreements made after the Gulf War, he is rearming his country.

Nostradamus sees the state of Israel as another part of the Middle East which will become destabilized.

Aux champs de Mede, d'Arabe & d'Armenie,
Deux grans copies trois fois s'assembleront:
Pres du rivage d'Araxes la mesgnie,
Du grand Soliman en terre tomberant.
CIII Q31

On the battlefields of Media, Arabia
  and Armenia,
Two great armies will assemble three times,
Near the shore of Araxes, the people,
Of great Soliman will be defeated.

The Jews ('the people of great Soliman') will be defeated three times in land battles in the Middle East near the coastal town of Araxes. Although the Arab–Israeli peace talks of 1992 and 1993 resulted in some degree of self-determination for the Palestinians in the Gaza Strip and discussions about the return of other Arab states continue, the spread of Islamic fundamentalism threatens to destabilize the whole of the Middle East. It also appears that Iran supports various terrorist groups eager for aggressive action against Israel.

Although Nostradamus foresees a defeat for Israel, he predicts her eventual victory.

Nouvelle loi terre neufve occuper,
Vers la Syrie, Judee & Palestine:
Le grand empire barbare corruer,
Avant que Phoebus son siecle determine.
CIII Q97

A new law will occupy a new land,
Around Syria, Judea and Palestine,
The great Barbarian empire will collapse,
Before the century of the sun has ended.

Here Nostradamus appears to be saying that, after losing the battles referred to in CIII Q31, Israel will emerge as the ultimate victor and occupy parts of Syria, Judea and Palestine. The 'great Barbarian empire' probably refers to those countries in the Middle East which are hostile to Israel, many now rallying under the Islamic fundamentalist banner. Israel has traditionally referred to her enemies as barbarians.

Nostradamus does not explain how the predominantly Arab empire in the Middle East will collapse, but it is interesting to note in this context that Israel has one of the largest stockpiles of nuclear weapons in the world. In the twentieth century, all countries possessing such weapons have been too afraid of the consequences of using them to risk doing so. Perhaps, if her people are threatened, Israel might resort to nuclear warfare to ensure her ultimate victory.

Above: Yasser Arafat, leader of the PLO, shakes the hand of the Israeli Prime Minister, Yitsak Rabin, watched over by a benevolent President Clinton after signing the Israel-PLO Peace Accord at the White House in Washington in 1994.

CIVIL WAR IN
YUGOSLAVIA

Above: Civilians run through the street in Sarajevo to avoid sniper fire from nearby buildings. Many thousands have been victims in the sectarian war of the Balkans that began in 1992.

THE PRIORITY OF the Yugoslav government during the 1980s was to reduce the country's soaring rate of inflation. In an increasingly economically unstable country, Serbian nationalists staged mass demonstrations and riots in 1988. The result has been a full-blown civil war.

Nostradamus predicts ethnic fighting in the former Yugoslavia.

Conflict Barbara en la Cornere noire,
Sang espandu trembler la d'Almatie.
CIX Q60

A barbarous fight in the black corner,
There will be bloodshed and Dalmatia shall
tremble with fear.

In the sixteenth century Dalmatia was an independent state on the Adriatic in the area now known as the former Yugoslavia. The scale of the brutality and bloodshed in the civil war between Serbs, Croats, Bosnians and Moslems prompted the United Nations to send armed convoys of relief supplies to assist the thousands of refugees whose homes had been destroyed. Of those who were unable to escape the depredations of their attackers, many fell victim to torture, rape, hunger and sickness; many died.

The true believers – as Muhammad called the Moslems – will suffer and die as a result of a religious war.

Voudrant loix sainctes injustement debatre,
Par foudre & guerre bien croyans à mort mis.
CIV Q43

They will wish unjustly to put down the Holy
Laws,
And by lightning and war, true believers will
be put to death.

The systematic slaughter of many Bosnian Moslems by non-Moslem Serbs, so-called ethnic cleansing, fulfilled Nostradamus's prophecy that the Holy Laws of the Moslems would come under threat. Still believing their lives to be in jeopardy because of the difficulties in reaching solutions to the conflict that satisfy the wishes and demands of all the factions in addition to the Serb violations of supposed peace agreements, the 'true believers' are demanding that the ban on the supply of arms to the Bosnian Moslems be lifted.

Right-wing political groups in Russia are now supporting the Bosnian Serbs, which may further endanger the lives of the region's Moslems.

Below: Huge new graveyards mark the civilian death toll of the brutal civil war and have become a familiar sight in Bosnia.

FINANCIAL COLLAPSE

NOSTRADAMUS was financially astute. He probably inherited a healthy respect for money from his Jewish ancestors who found themselves forced into commerce and moneylending in states which forbade them many occupations. His first published works, the yearly almanacs, gave predictions and advice on many practical matters, including astrological indications of the most favourable times for financial or business dealings. There were also many townsfolk in Salon who would make no commercial decisions without first consulting *'le prophète'*. It is not surprising, therefore, that in the *Centuries* Nostradamus focuses on the wider financial horizons of the future.

Nostradamus sees a bleak outlook for the world's financial future, predicting that inflation will be the scourge of the late twentieth century, and will be followed by bankruptcy on a global scale.

Right: What future lies ahead for the dollar?

Far right: A cutting from the *New York Times* of Wednesday, 30th October 1929 announces the Wall Street Crash which prompted a number of suicides by those unable to face the loss of everything they owned. It was followed by a slump which affected the economies of all western industrialized countries.

Les simulacres d'or & argent enflez,
Qu'apres le rapt au lac furent gettez
Au desouvert estaincts tous & troublez,
Au marbre script prescript intergetez.
CVIII Q28

Simulations of gold and silver are inflated,
Which after the theft are thrown into the lake
*   of fire,*
At the discovery that all is consumed and
*   wasted by the debt,*
All share certificates and bonds shall be
*   cancelled.*

It is interesting to note the reference to paper money (copies or simulations of gold and silver) which did not exist at the time Nostradamus wrote this quatrain. The second line of the quatrain is not easy to interpret although there is a suggestion that it refers to the fortunes plundered by the Nazis during the Second World War and never recovered. The last two lines appear to sum up the financial future, when public debts will be so great that all investments, represented by paper certificates, will become worthless.

Inflation (a depreciation in the value of money) has been a feature of most Western economies in the twentieth century, particularly since the Second World War. There are several remedies to counter inflation, all of which have been tried at some time or another in the last fifty years. They include raising

Above: New York's army of unemployed is illustrated here in a demonstration during the Great Depression of the 1930s.

taxes; altering interest rates; controlling government spending; limiting the money supply; and introducing a prices and incomes policy. One of the aims of the British government, and others, is to control inflation, largely through interest rate changes and government spending controls. As a result, many businesses – which rely on bank loans to start up and keep running – have been unable to repay loans when interest rates rise. As companies fail, so unemployment rises and as fewer people pay taxes, the economic recovery has another setback. The present global economic situation reflects the relevance of Nostradamus's words.

Nostradamus focuses his attention on one of the world's main banking systems and predicts that Switzerland will be involved in financial scandal and that her secret bank neutrality will be broken.

Below: Throughout the eighties, Japan's economy expanded at an incredible rate. By the end of the decade, the Tokyo Stock Exchange was the world's largest securities exchange.

La republique miserable infelice
Sera vastee de nouveau magistrat:
Leur grand amus de l'exile malefice,
Fera Sueve ravir leur grand contracts.
CI Q61

The wretched, unfortunate republic,
Will again be ruined by a new authority:
The great amount of bad feeling developed
* in exile,*
Will make the Swiss break their important
* agreement.*

Switzerland will be shamed when it is proved that her banks are involved in stockpiling and laundering money and gold for international criminal organizations. Switzerland's application for full membership of the European Union will mean, according to E. U. regulations, that the Swiss banks' established code of neutrality would be broken, forcing them to reveal their accounts for inspection. Such a change, Nostradamus suggests, would cause a great deal of international bad feeling among wealthy and powerful investors who could exert pressure on the Swiss banks to break their 'important agreement', that is the E. U. rules of membership.

Nostradamus warns of the disaster that will follow when the spending of prosperous countries gets out of control.

Le grand credit d'or, d'argent l'abondance
Fera aveugler par libide honneur
Sera cogneu d'adultere l'offense
Qui parviendra à son grand deshonneur.
CVIII Q14

The great reserves of gold and abundance of
   silver,
Will cause honour to be blinded by greed,
The offence of the adulterer will become known,
Which shall be a great dishonour to him.

The situation which Nostradamus describes here has already happened as the end of the millennium approaches. He saw the worship of materialism and the cult of the acquisitive society leading to a breakdown of moral standards in general. The implication of the quatrain is the association of material and financial greed with sexual lust which will result in a morally degenerate society. To Nostradamus's sixteenth-century mind 'honour' was under attack – a concept which may have less currency in late-twentieth-century thinking.

Above: Paper money from around the world symbolizes the fragile interconnected nature of the world's money markets which Nostradamus dwelled on in his writings.

Left: The main banking district in Zurich, Switzerland is one of the world's most important centres for banking and insurance. The unique attraction of Swiss banking is its secrecy rules which protect the confidentiality of clients and their transactions.

THE END OF THE BRITISH MONARCHY?

PEOPLE HAVE ALWAYS required that their royalty are surrounded by the mystique of fairytale and romance. For the most part – at least in the modern era – the British royal family has been happy to fulfil this requirement and, in return, its members have conducted themselves, whatever their private difficulties, in a manner which does not bring them into public disrepute. Princes and princesses may marry but, as in all good fairytales, they must live happily ever after. To do otherwise is to risk the stability of the monarchy itself.

On 9th December 1992, British Prime Minister John Major made the following statement to M.P.s in the House of Commons: 'It is announced from Buckingham Palace, that, with regret, the Prince and Princess of Wales have decided to separate. Their Royal Highnesses have no plans to divorce and their constitutional positions are unaffected. Their decision has been reached amicably, and they will both continue to participate fully in the upbringing of their children. Their Royal Highnesses will continue to carry out full and separate programmes of public engagements, and will from

Right: The famous balcony kiss between Prince Charles and his new bride Diana, Princess of Wales, sealed the myth of their fairytale romance.

time to time attend family occasions and national events together. The Queen and the Duke of Edinburgh, though saddened, understand and sympathize with the difficulties that have led to this decision ... [and] particularly hope that the intrusions into the privacy of the Prince and Princess may now cease. They believe that a degree of privacy and understanding is essential if Their Royal Highnesses are to provide a happy and secure upbringing for their children, while continuing to give a wholehearted commitment to their public duties.'

Although it might seem extraordinary that a sixteenth-century French seer should predict the fortunes of the twentieth-century British royal family, Nostradamus was a staunch royalist and had made prophetic comment on other occasions about monarchies which came to grief. Is it not likely that he would have had

particular interest in the monarchy of a country for which he predicted such a great and glorious future (see pages 78–9)?

Nostradamus predicts the breakdown of the marriage of the Prince and Princess of Wales and the end of the monarchy itself.

Vent chaud, conseil, pleurs, timidite,
De nuict au lit assailly sans les armes,
D'oppression grand calamite,
L'Epithalame converty pleurs & larmes.
CVII Q83

Hot wind, counsel, tears, fearfulness,
He shall be assaulted in his bed by night
*   without arms,*
From that oppression shall be raised a great
*   calamity,*
The Epithalamium shall be converted into tears.

Above: The British Royal Family pictured on Her Majesty, the Queen's 39th birthday in 1965, a time when a sense of mystique still surrounded the monarchy and the public were only permitted rare and unobtrusive glimpses into family life.

The last line provides the clue to the subject matter of this quatrain. The Epithalamium is a wedding song or poem (*thalamion* is Greek for the bridal chamber). Here the word can be interpreted as the much publicized celebration of the marriage of Prince Charles and Lady Diana Spencer in July 1981. In that context, the first line clearly depicts the quarrels between Charles and Diana, the discussions between Diana and her friends, her intimates' revelations of her frequent tears and Diana's own fearfulness of her inability to cope with the demands and stresses of her position, admitted with the publication of Andrew Morton's book, *Diana: Her True Story.*

Nostradamus foresees the difficulties of this marriage. The potent imagery of the second line is a reference to the nightmarish effect on Prince Charles of Diana's accusations. He declines to defend himself in public against this attack. The prophet also predicts that the mutual misery of Charles and Diana, and their inevitable separation and divorce, will cause this marriage to end unhappily.

Right: Camilla Parker Bowles chats to Prince Charles at a polo match in the 1970s. The breakdown of his marriage followed by the Prince's admission of adultery has rocked the institution of the British monarchy and may have jeopardised his right to succeed to the throne.

Left: The Prince and Princess of Wales on a royal visit to Korea in 1992. The couple displayed open discord throughout the trip and formally announced their separation soon afterward.

The future of Charles, the heir to the throne, is of concern to Nostradamus, although there is no way to tell how far into the future he is looking with this quatrain.

Le jeune nay au regne Britannique,
Qu'aurale pere mourant recommandé,
Icelui mort LONOLE donra topique,
Et à son fils le regne demandé.
CX Q40

The young man born to the kingdom of Britain,
Whom his dying father shall have
*   recommended,*
After his death, London shall give him a topic,
And the kingdom will be demanded back from
*   the son.*

As Prince Philip, the Queen's consort, is dying he urges Charles to succeed to the throne of Great Britain on the death of his mother, Queen Elizabeth II. The constitutional crisis that will occur if Charles and Diana are divorced at this time is a matter of speculation. Although the meaning of this quatrain is not altogether clear, the implication is that Charles will never be king. A regency until Prince William comes of age could be the offer made to him by London (Parliament). The last line of the quatrain suggests that the United Kingdom chooses a republic as its form of government by 'demanding the kingdom back from the son'.

Below: Headlines such as this one from the *Daily Mirror* of Wednesday, 2nd June 1993 portray a monarchy in crisis.

DAILY **Mirror**

40 GLORIOUS YEARS?
ROYAL SOUVENIR INSIDE

Wednesday, June 2, 1993   INSIDE: 4-PAGE DERBY PULL-OUT   27p

HOW LONG TO REIGN OVER US?

THE MIRROR ASKS THE CRUCIAL QUESTION ON THE QUEEN'S ANNIVERSARY

Illustration: CHARLES GRIFFIN

FORTY years ago today Elizabeth Alexandra Mary was crowned Queen of the United Kingdom, head of the Commonwealth and Defender of the Faith.

The *Daily Mirror* congratulates Her Majesty on this latest milestone in her

MIRROR COMMENT

is no coincidence that she has insisted there shall be no official celebrations.

There will be gun salutes at Hyde Park and the Tower of London. And that is all. The Queen will visit The Derby, as usual, and will spend the

evening alone at Windsor. Not even her family will be with her.

Some anniversary.

Yet that is hardly surprising. For British Royalty is in crisis. Its greatest crisis since the Abdication of 1936. A crisis mainly of its own making.

As the Queen looks back on the 40 years of her reign she will wonder where

TURN TO PAGE 6

GLOBAL FAMINE
AND CANNIBALISM

Right: Starving children in the Sudan stretch out their hungry hands. Many Third World countries now rely on the constant supply of international food aid, even when the harvest is good, in order to satisfy the overwhelming needs of their population growth.

Opposite page: The world's attention has recently been drawn again to the plight of Somalia. Civil war and the huge scale looting by gunmen of relief supplies has exacerbated existing food shortages and created mass starvation shown here in disturbing detail.

NOSTRADAMUS saw food shortages as one of the worst problems facing the world at the end of the 1990s. Scientific evidence in many cases links famine with man's own activities. Extensive forests are being cut down and burned to clear land for agriculture, for mineral exploitation and for raw materials used in the construction, furniture and paper industries. This has several major effects: without tree roots to help anchor it to the ground, topsoil is liable to erode, which makes crops more likely to fail. The reduction of water in the soil means that there is less water in the atmosphere, which makes rainfall less likely with the result that drought may follow. Deprived of rainfall for their crops, populations of areas which are affected by deforestation quickly fall prey to famine.

Nostradamus predicts the approach of a universal famine of such long duration that it would constitute a worldwide disaster.

La grande famine que je sens approcher,
Souvent tourner, puis estre universelle:
Si grand & long qu'un viendra arracher,
Du bois racine & l'enfant de mamelle
CI Q67

The great famine that I sense drawing near,
Often moving from one country to another and
then becoming universal,
So great and so long that they will come to
pluck,
The root from the wood and the child from the
breast.

Over the past ten years, television pictures have transmitted horrifying scenes of the misery caused by famine in Ethiopia, the Sudan, Somalia, Rwanda and India. The graphic imagery of the last two lines of the quatrain is commonplace in many parts of Africa. Film coverage has revealed the desperate attempts of the starving to ward off hunger by feeding on roots of decaying trees and the miserable plight of infants clinging to their mothers' empty breasts until they die through lack of sustenance.

Indian author Kamala Markandaya evokes the personal horror and pain of hunger: '... at first it is with you all the time, waking and sleeping and in your dreams, and your belly cries out insistently, and there is a gnawing and a pain as if your very vitals were being devoured .... Then the pain is no longer sharp but dull, and this too is with you always, so that you think of food many times a day .... Then that too is gone, all pain, all desire, only a great emptiness is left, like the sky, like a well in drought, and it is now that the strength drains from your limbs, and you try to rise and find you cannot, or to swallow water and your throat is powerless, and both the swallow and the effort of retaining the liquid tax you to the uttermost.'

Nostradamus predicts a great catastrophe when wealth-creating countries are no longer able to give aid to countries in economic trouble, and themselves become victims of poverty and food shortages.

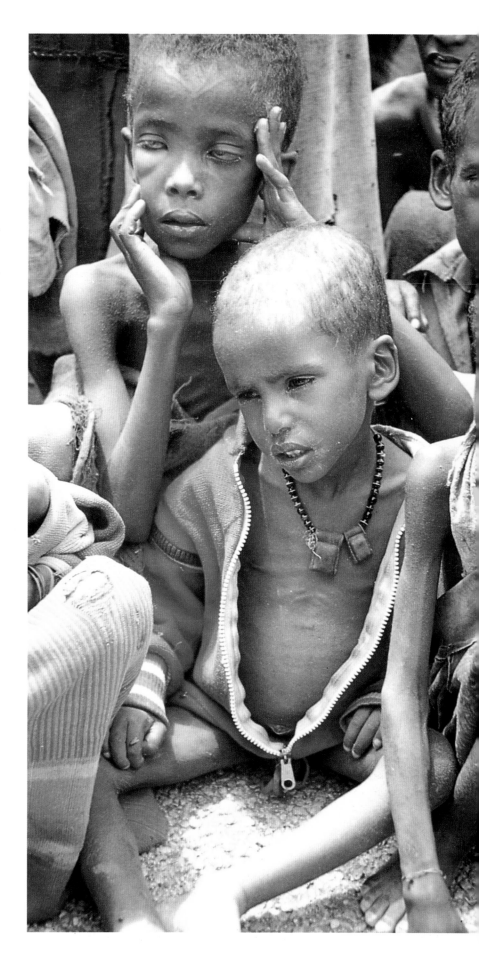

La pitie grande sera loing tarder,
Ceux qui donoient seront contrains de prendre.
Nudz affamez de froit, soif, soi bander,
Les monts passer commettant grand esclandre.
CVI Q69

It will be a great pity that before very long
Those who gave shall be forced to take,
Naked, hungry, cold and thirsty [they will be
driven] to mutiny,
By going over the mountains making great
trouble.

Nostradamus foresees with sorrow the imminent starvation facing the inhabitants of those countries which currently have substantial food reserves. Studies of the significance of climatic change indicate that such a calamity could occur at the end of this century. At the beginning of the 1990s meteorologists forecast that weather patterns will alter dramatically over the last eight years of this century, predicting long periods of severe cold with no rainfall which will result in long droughts and disastrously affect world food production.

Surplus grain grown in the 'bread basket' states of the U. S. has traditionally fed the peoples of the Soviet republics and many Third World countries. Any large crop failure will have a devastating effect on these people. The European Union, renowned for its stockpiles of food, will also be affected by global changes in climate, reducing its capacity to provide emergency food aid to the Third World and ultimately to feed its own increasing populations. In this quatrain, too, Nostradamus sees world food shortages as a cause of civil and international strife. Refugees from famine will inevitably move into other countries as their own resources become exhausted. This situation will often be exacerbated by local wars (this is already contributing to famine in parts of Africa).

Below: The vast prairies of the American mid-west produce over half the world's supply of wheat.

There are several references to cannibalism in the *Centuries*, both linked to Nostradamus's prophecies on famine and as a subject to stand alone.

Famine and the escalating price of basic food-stuffs such as grain could eventually lead to cannibalism.

La voix ouie de l'insolite oiseau,
Sur le carron de respiral estage:
Si hault viendra du froment le boisseau,
Quel'homme de l'homme fera Antropophage.
CII Q75

The call of the unwanted bird
on the chimney stack,
A basket of wheat will reach such a high
*   price,*
That man will eat his fellow man.

In this rather obscure quatrain Nostradamus again forecasts food shortages, rampant inflation and the desperate measures to which starving humans resort. Ritual cannibalism was once practised by several peoples, including the Maori of New Zealand and the Carib Indians, but eating human flesh is generally taboo and only undertaken in extreme circumstances. It was an accepted practice among shipwreck survivors until the nineteenth century to draw lots to decide who should be sacrificed to save the rest and it reputedly occurred in the concentration camps during the Second World War. There is also a well-documented example of the survivors of a plane crash in the Andes mountains in 1972 eating the flesh of their dead companions in order to stay alive.

The unwanted bird on the chimney stack, who gives the warning in the last line, is a crow or raven, both traditionally birds of ill omen.

Above: Stranded in the icy mountains for many days, the survivors of the aircrash in the Andes, Argentina in 1972 had to eat the flesh of their dead companions to sustain themselves while they waited to be rescued.

NATURAL DISASTERS

THE PROPHECIES of Nostradamus are greatly concerned with calamitous events. In the style of the Biblical prophets he sometimes attributes particular calamities to human wrong-doing (he believed, for example, that the Great Plague of London was a punishment for the execution of Charles I, CII Q53), although throughout the *Centuries* he also predicts large-scale disasters on national and global scales without giving any reason or explanation for their occurrence.

Nostradamus's religious background meant that he would, in all likelihood, have accepted the theory put forward in both the Old and New Testaments that the arrival of each millennium brought with it unprecedented disasters.

To the astonishment of many commentators the year 1000 arrived with no signal catastrophes. Foreboding was then transferred to the second millennium which Nostradamus sees with great clarity as a time of unprecedented misfortune and major change ('Plague, famine, death at the hand of warriors – the century approaches renewal', CI Q16).

Nostradamus refers to the specific location of future disasters, foreseeing that there will be severe flooding in Great Britain.

La grande Bretagne comprinse l'Angleterre,
Viendra par eaux si haut a inonder ...
CIII Q70

Great Britain including England,
Will suffer great inundations of water ...

It is interesting that Nostradamus here refers to Great Britain although at the time of making the prediction the unification of the English and Scottish thrones under James I (James VI of Scotland) in 1603, had not taken place. Likewise the term 'Great Britain' was not coined until that time.

A rise in sea levels of only a few centimetres, a real possibility according to scientists studying the effects of global warming, would severely affect many areas of Great Britain, including the Southeast, Humberside and East Anglia, which are at or close to sea level. The cost of strengthening sea defences against a rise of around one metre in these vulnerable areas was estimated in the early 1990s at some £5 billion. A tidal barrier across the river Thames in London, in anticipation of raised water levels in the course of the next decade, was completed in 1983.

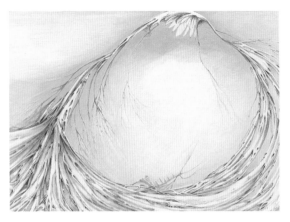

Left: 'The Dying Planet'. Planet Earth, hot and dry, roots struggling for moisture is Dario Poli's view of the effect of climatic change on our future world.

A tidal wave and massive flooding are predicted for an American coastal city.

Jardin du monde au pres du cité neufve,
Dans le chemin des montaignes cavees,
Sera saisi & plongé dans la Cuve,
Beuvant par force eaux soulfre envenimees.
CX Q49

Garden of the world, near the New City
In the way of manmade mountains,
Will be seized and plunged into ferment,
Forced to drink water poisoned with sulphur.

Left: The Thames Flood Barrier at Woolwich. Fears that the city could be innundated by rare 'surge tides' thrust up the estuary by North Sea gales, prompted the London authorities to erect downstream barriers which became fully operational in 1983.

This terrible catastrophe will occur in a place which is identified by its gardens and manmade mountains (skyscrapers) near the New City (this has to be New York, founded by Dutch colonists in the 1620s as New Amsterdam, capital of New Netherland). These clues pinpoint the site of this disaster as Atlantic City, noted for its towering skyline and situated in the 'garden state' of New Jersey. The quatrain appears to describe a huge tidal wave from the Atlantic Ocean flooding the city with sulphurous chemicals which contaminate the drinking water system.

Nostradamus predicts a major earthquake for San Francisco in April.

Au fondement de la nouvelle secte,
Seront les os du grand Romain trouvés,
Sepulchre en marbre apparoistra couverte,
Terre trembler en Avril, mal enfouetz.
CVI Q66

At the founding of a new sect,
The bones of the great Roman will be found,
A sepulchre covered in marble will appear,
The earth will quake in April.

Below: Atlantic City's precarious position on a thin island separated from the US mainland by a narrow strait and several miles of meadow which are covered with water at high tide, makes it an easy target for the ocean.

This quatrain is obscure and its interpretation requires ingenuity. The second and third lines indicate a historical Roman or Italian figure of some repute who, as is suggested by the marble tomb, has achieved immortality. Taken as a whole the quatrain could refer to the Italian, Francis of Assisi, who achieved immortality through being canonized in 1228 (he has also been the patron saint of ecology since 1980). This sites the earthquake in San Francisco, which was founded by an order of Franciscan monks.

San Francisco was built on the San Andreas Fault, a 1,200-km fault in the earth's crust where the North America plate (on which most of the continent sits) and the Pacific plate (on which the narrow coastal strip of northwestern California and the Pacific Ocean sit) meet. Friction between the plates causes earth movements which range from slight tremors to intense volcanic activity. The city of San Francisco was completely destroyed by an earthquake and subsequent fire in 1906, but rebuilt on the same site. San Francisco is marked out by Nostradamus for a spectacular 'quake' in the month of April, although the year is not specified and American volcanologists and seismologists also have no definite forecasts of any future disturbance of the earth's surface in this area. The last major quake in the city was in 1989, in October, not April.

Nostradamus also foresees a cataclysmic earthquake for 10th May. Although again he does not provide an exact date, it is evident that this devastating event has not yet occurred and may well be a part of the global mayhem he saw as heralding the millennium.

Sol vingt de Taurus si fort terre trembler,
Le grand theatre rempli ruinera,
L'air ciel & terre obscurcir & troubler
Lors l'infidelle Dieu & sainctz voguera.
CIX Q83

Left: A bridge collapses during the San Francisco earthquake of 1989. Despite its precarious position on the San Andreas Fault line, millions of people continue to inhabit a city which has already been demolished by one earthquake, and whose future, according to Nostradamus, is equally bleak.

The sun in twenty degrees of Taurus, there will be a great earthquake,
That it will fill and ruin the great theatre,
The air, the sky and the earth will be so dark and troubled,
That unbelievers will call upon God and the saints.

This earthquake will be so violent that it will shake the foundations of the world. The disturbance of the plates under the earth's crust, which move as a result of turbulence deep within its core, will cause continents to be riven apart and new oceans to appear between the new continental land masses. The 'great theatre' is a metaphor for the whole world which, at the moment of catastrophe, will be plunged into darkness. Even those who have no faith will call upon their God to help them in their great terror.

THE THIRD
ANTICHRIST AND
THIRD WORLD WAR

J EWISH BY RACE, but baptized a Catholic as a result of the religious climate into which he was born, Nostradamus believed in the Biblical prophecies of Armageddon and the Antichrist. The last judgement, the overthrow of a current corrupt order in favour of a more enlightened one, was in Christian tradition more likely to occur at the end of a millennium – a thousand-year period measured from the birth of Christ (there was widespread panic in Europe as the last day of AD 999 approached midnight). In accordance with sixteenth-

Right: Hitler, the second of Nostradamus's predicted antichrists visits the tomb of the first antichrist, Napoleon Bonaparte, in 1940.

century Christian thinking, and the teaching of many fundamentalist preachers and scholars today, Nostradamus believed that having survived one millennium, the world may not be so lucky a second time.

Nostradamus predicted the arrival of not one but three Antichrists (people whose teachings are opposed to those of Christ). Most interpreters of the *Centuries* consider that the first Antichrist was Napoleon Bonaparte, who Nostradamus depicts as one of the most destructive human beings of his age, a usurper of the French throne and a ruthless and arrogant butcher. The second Antichrist is generally understood to be Adolf Hitler, whose downfall Nostradamus saw clearly. The third Antichrist is yet to come. Nostradamus had an apocalyptic vision of the end of the twentieth century which he depicted in many of his quatrains. The fact that he dated so few of his predictions serves to heighten the significance of any date that does appear.

One of the most significant dates in the *Centuries* is the year 1999 when Nostradamus predicts the arrival of a third and terrible Antichrist from the East.

> *L'an mil neuf cens nonante neuf sept mois,*
> *Du ciel viendra un grand Roi deffraieur.*
> *Resusciter le grand Roi d'Angolmois.*
> *Avant que Mars regner par bonheur.*
> CX Q72

> *In the year 1999 and seven months,*
> *From the skies will come a great King of Terror,*
> *To bring back life to the great King of the*
>   *Mongols,*
> *Before and after war will reign at will.*

The prospect for the human race as the prophet explains his vision of the millennium's approach, is laden with doom. Nostradamus foresees a catastrophic war taking place preceding and following the arrival in July 1999 of

Above: In many parts of the world religious fervour has increased as the end of the twentieth century draws to a close. An example of this is expressed here by the self flagellation of moslem fundamentalists.

a supremely powerful and terrifying figure from the East. This awe-inspiring being will reinstate the Antichrist from Asia (King of the Mongols) by giving him support (probably weapons and arms) so that war will occur on a massive scale.

The arrival of this leader will signal the outbreak of the Third World War. He will attack and annihilate three leaders whose nations will collapse with them. This act of belligerence will unleash a war of vengeance against him which will last twenty-seven years.

> *L'antichrist trois bien tost anniehilez,*
> *Vingt & sept ans sang durera sa guerre,*
> *Les heretiques mortz, captifs, exilez.*
> *Sang corps humain eau rougi gresler terre.*
> CVIII Q77

> *The Antichrist very soon wipes out the three,*
> *His war will last twenty-seven years,*
> *The unbelievers are dead, captive or exiled,*
> *Blood, human body, water turned red, and the*
> *   earth shrivelled.*

By skilful strategy and force of armaments the Antichrist defeats the opposition. Some are killed, others are taken captive, leaving huge numbers to flee as refugees. The 'shrivelled earth' in the last line suggests a devastated world drained of its vital life force. (Or is this a reference to the aftermath of a nuclear explosion, when all that remains of cities and forests are charred ruins, and since the smoke from the fires has blackened the sun, temperatures fall and crops fail?) In his vision Nostradamus sees that rivers and oceans will run red with the blood of the slaughtered.

In the 1990s vast areas of Asia from the fringes of Europe to Mongolia have become politically unstable through war or revolution. Ethnic wars continue in the former Yugoslavia; Kurds and Shia Moslems are persecuted in Iraq; and there are civil wars being waged in Azerbaijan and Afghanistan. Opposing factions in Cambodia make a renewed outbreak of hostilities there likely and the death of Kim Il Sung, President of North Korea, in 1994, has further destabilized the Korean peninsula.

Above and below: A Tomahawk Cruise Missile swoops down from the sky and obliterates its target. The precise navigational systems of modern weapons are now so sophisicated and lethal, we hold the power to completely destroy the planet. Life as we know it is unlikely survive a Third World War.

Nostradamus reinforces his forecast of doom for the end of the twentieth century.

> *Faulx à l'estang joint vers le Sagitaire,*
> *Enson hault AUGE de l'exaltation,*
> *Peste, famine, mort de main militaire,*
> *La siecle approche de renouvation.*
> CI Q16

> *A scythe joined with a pool when Sagittarius*
> *is at the zenith of its ascendancy,*
> *Plague, famine, from military hands,*
> *The century approaches its renewal.*

This quatrain echoes CX Q72 in suggesting a climactic War of Wars in 1999 when a scythe (the sign of Saturn) is in conjunction with a pool (the water sign, Aquarius) and Sagittarius is at its highest point in the heavens. The reference to renewal clearly indicates the end of the century and could suggest the ancient esoteric tradition of a dawning age of Aquarius in which the corrupt materialistic order is replaced with spiritual ideals. Nostradamus is unusually specific here. The age of Aquarius will begin in the early twenty-first century and last approximately 1,500 years. It supercedes the Piscean age which will last from around 950 BC to AD 2050. The naming of Sagittarius as the ascendant planet places this destructive war between 23rd November and 21st December. If Nostradamus is viewed in the great tradition of Biblical prophets his words may be warnings which, in the fields of human rights, international politics, ecology and even ethics, we ignore at our peril.

Left: The towering statue of Kim Il Sung, President of the People's Democratic Republic of Korea, who died in 1994. A powerful communist leader from the east, Kim Il Sung dominated Korean policies from almost half a century. A potential antichrist figure, he did not fulfil the role predicted by Nostradamus.

Below: The arrival of the Third Antichrist, harbinger of millenial terror, by Dario Poli.

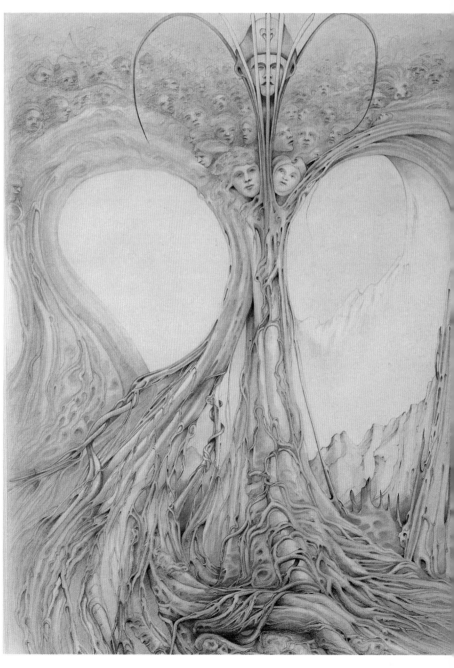

FUTURE PEACE

MANY COMMENTATORS choose to focus on the pessimism of the *Centuries* which at times seem to be a relentless catalogue of the misfortunes befalling kings and queens and the collapse of the established orders, in addition to wars, famine and pestilence. His prophetic works, however, are not all in such a dark vein.

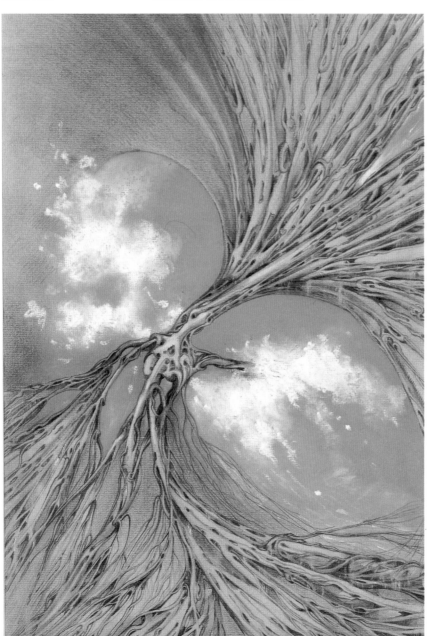

Below: 'View into Space' a scene of tranquility and enlightenment by Dario Poli.

Toward the end of the *Centuries* Nostradamus predicts a time when mankind's aggressive instincts will eventually disappear.

La fin le loup, le lyon, beuf & l'asne,
Timide dama seront avec mastins,
Plus ne charra à eux la douce manne,
Plus vigilance & custode aux mastins.
CX Q99

In the end the wolf, the lion, ox and ass,
The gentle deer, will lie down with the mastiffs,
No longer will the sweet manna fall to them,
There will be no more guarding and keeping of
*   mastiffs.*

He uses Biblical imagery here to describe his vision of peace after centuries of bloodshed and war. Once warring nations stop fighting each other, food ('sweet manna') will no longer be in the control of strong, powerful groups or nations. In view of news coverage of the appalling effects of famine in many parts of the world, international aid agencies at least are beginning to advocate that enabling the hungry to feed themselves is almost certainly preferable to giving food aid on an *ad hoc* basis. Nostradamus also envisages an end to the arming of nations and the stockpiling of weapons, suggesting an end to wars. Perhaps there is a correlation between the two: when people are not engaged in fighting each other, they can concentrate on feeding themselves and their families. And, if only a small percentage of the money spent on weapons technology were released for reforestation, irrigation, soil improvement and halting the relentless spread of the deserts, perhaps future wars could be avoided completely.

Future peace is confirmed by Nostradamus, but it is merely a part of the inevitable cycle of war and peace.

> *Les fleurs passés diminue le monde,*
> *Longtemps la paix terres inhabités:*
> *Seur marchera par ciel, serre, mer & onde:*
> *Puis de nouveau les guerres suscitées.*
> CI Q63

> *Pestilences being finished, the world will be*
>   *made smaller,*
> *For a long time lands will be at peace but*
>   *uninhabited,*
> *Everyone will go safely by air, land and sea:*
> *Then wars will begin anew.*

The populations of the world will be decimated by war, famine and disease so that many countries will be more or less uninhabited. At the same time, the world will appear smaller as a result of the development of communications, especially travel from one part of the globe to the other by modern transport (this situates the quatrain firmly in the twentieth century and beyond). The emphasis which Nostradamus places on the safety of travel is clearly a reference to the hazards of travel in his own day. He must have been amazed at seeing the ease with which travellers could hop continents with a minimum of discomfort and danger.

He predicts, however, that peace will not last. It seems part of the inexorable cycle of history – and the last line of the quatrain makes this clear – that in periods of peace, war is dormant and simply waiting to be unleashed.

Above: Scenes of breathtaking beauty and infinite calm are one of two alternatives suggested by Nostradamus for the new millennium. The outcome is for us to decide.

THE END OF THE WORLD

NOSTRADAMUS'S visions of the future are always visions of great change. He returns many times throughout the *Centuries* to the horrors and terrible tragedies that await humanity.

Nostradamus's vision of the future is one of an excess of horror and war.

> *Vous verrez tost & tard taire grand change,*
> *Horreurs extremes, & vindications:*
> *Que si la lune conduicte par son ange,*
> *Le ciel s'approche des inclinations.*
> C1 Q56

> *Sooner or later you will see great changes made,*
> *Dreadful horrors and vengeances,*
> *As the moon is led by her angel,*
> *The heaven draws near its inclination.*

Perhaps, in the manner of the Biblical prophets, Nostradamus believed that human folly could be averted so long as the human race was given sufficient warning and was wise enough to heed it and change its ways. It seems, however, that no matter where Nostradamus looked into the future, his faith was unjustified.

Left: 'Apocalypse'. Dario Poli's premonition of the future calamity of mankind. The image of the central conflict was inspired by the Battle of Solferino on 24th June 1859 – an indecisive, bloody battle, in which 30,000 people lost their lives.

The last two lines of the quatrain point to the role of astrology in Nostradamus's predictions. He believes that the earth's destruction will come about when the moon and planets are in a certain (unspecified) relationship to each other. The use of the word 'inclinations' in the last line of the quatrain may be a reference to the 'balance', the astrological symbol for Libra.

Nostradamus predicts the end of the world in the year 7000 when the sun will destroy the earth and regain its place of supreme power in the universe.

Vingt ans de la regne de la lune passez,
Sept mil ans autre tiendra sa monarchie
Quand le soleil prendra ses jours lassez,
Lors accomplit & mine ma prophetie.
CI Q48

When twenty years of the reign of the moon
*   have passed,*
In 7000 years another shall take up his
*   reign,*
When the sun resumes his exhausted cycle,
Then my prophecy is fulfilled and ended.

It was a widely held belief in the Middle Ages, based on apocalyptic verses in the Book of Enoch, that human history would last for 7,000 years. (The Book of Enoch – in fact there were two, the first of which contains the apocalyptic visions - was general reading until AD 300 when it was removed from the Church canon largely because it was proven not to have been written by him but by several Jewish authors in the second century BC.)

The major difficulty with this quatrain is in calculating when to start counting the 7,000 years. If we accept that Nostradamus thought that the birth of Christ should be the start date, then the world will end in about 5,000 years time. There is, however, no proof that Nostradamus did take this as his start date.

St John, in Revelations, also referred to the seventh millennium as heralding a 'new age', although elsewhere in the New Testament (Matthew 24; Mark 13; Luke 21) statements about the end of mankind and Christ's second coming indicate that the exact time of these events is impossible to know or calculate. John also names the site of the last great battle between the forces of good and evil – a place called Armageddon.

Bibliography

Arkel, L. & Blake, D., *Nostradamus: The Final Countdown*, 1993

Barzini, L., *The Italians*, 1991

Boulenger, J., *Nostradamus, etc.*, 1933

Brennan, J. H., *Nostradamus: Visions of the Future*, 1992

Cheetham, E. (ed.), *The Further Prophecies of Nostradamus*, 1991

Cheetham, E. (ed.), *The Prophecies of Nostradamus*, 1981 (rev. ed.)

Edwards, F., *Flying Saucers Serious Business*, 1967

Francis, D. P., *Nostradamus: Prophecies of Present Times*, 1984

Fontbrune de, J. C., *Nostradamus: Countdown to the Apocalypse*, 1984

Hewitt, V. J. and Lorie, P., *Nostradamus: The End of the Millennium*, 1991

Hogue, J., *Nostradamus and the Millennium*, 1987

Laver, J., *Nostradamus or the Future Foretold*, 1981

Lorie, P. & Greene, L., *Nostradamus: The Millennium and Beyond*, 1993

Noorbergen, R., *Invitation to a Holocaust: Nostradamus forecasts World War III*, 1981

Petrucelli, L., *Medicine: An Illustrated History*, 1978

Ridge, M., *Nostradamus: An Illustrated Guide to his Predictions*, 1993

Roberts, H. C. (ed.), *Nostradamus: Complete Prophecies*, 1985 (3rd ed.)

Seligman, K., *The History of Magic*, 1948

Stewart, R. J., *Elements of Prophecy*, 1990

Voldben, A., *After Nostradamus*, 1973

Ward, C. A., *Oracles of Nostradamus*, 1986

Wasserman, J., *Art and Symbols of the Occult*, 1993

Picture Acknowledgements

AKG London: 82 (left), 82 (right) (Jacques Bertaux *Storming the Tuileries*, Versailles), 83 (F. Bouchot *Bonaparte in the Parliament of the Five Hundred at Saint-Cloud*, Versailles), 84 (L. F. Lejeune *The Battle of Aboukir*, Versailles), 88 (Elisabeth Heddenhausen), 89;
The Bodleian Library, Oxford: 8 (MS Ashmole 971 fol. 76v), 24 (bottom) (MS Canon Liturg 283 fol. 4), 24 (top right) (MS Douce 112 fol. 79), 30 (MS Canon Liturg 283 fol. 11), 32 (right) (MS Barocci 170 fol. 8v), 40 (MS Digby 46 fol. 52), 52 (MS Ashmole 1461 fol. 15r), 54 (right) (MS Canon Liturg 283 fol. 70v), 55 (top left & bottom right) & 57 (top) (MS Douce 112 fol. 121v), 55 (bottom left) (MS Douce 112 fol. 33), 57 (bottom) (MS Ashmole 1461 fol. 25v);
Bridgeman Art Library, London: 2 (T. Wijck *The Alchemist*, Johnny Van Haeften Gallery), 12 (Anon. *Planetary Trajectories*, National Museum, Stockholm), 18 (Fitzwilliam Museum, Cambridge), 51 (N. Hilliard *Queen Elizabeth I* (the Pelican Portrait), Walker Art Gallery, Liverpool), 72 (Dutch School *Charles I at a Cock Fight*, Rafael Vals Gallery, London), 75 (W. Vaillant *Charles II*, Phillips the Fine Art Auctioneers), 77 (L. Verschuter *Great Fire of London, 1666*, Museum of Fine Arts, Budapest), 81 (J-J. Hauer *Farewell to Louis XVI*, Musee de la Ville de Paris, Musee Carnavalet, Giraudon);
Jean-Loup Charmet, Paris: 14 (top & bottom), 16 (bottom right), 20 (bottom), 21, 22, 25, 26 (right), 31 (top & bottom), 33, 39, 43 (bottom), 44, 50 (top), 54 (left), 60, 61 (top right), 62 (right), 63, 64, 65, 68, 69, 73 (right), 80, 85 (Workshop of David *Coronation of Napoleon*, Collection Comedie Francaise);
ET Archive, London: 9 (*Nostradamus after Caesar*, Musee de Versailles), 46 (Biblioteca Estense, Modena), 59 (French School *Ball at the Court of Henry III*, Louvre, Paris), 61 (bottom left) (Ingres *Sword of Henry IV Kissed by Pedro of Toledo*, Louvre, Paris), 87 (left) (Callot *Louis Pasteur Examines Fermentation in Wine*, Pasteur Birthplace, Dole), 100 (right), 102 (left), 119 (top), 134;
Daily Mirror/John Frost Newspapers, London: 110 (top), 125 (bottom);
Hulton Deutsch Collection, London: 79 (top left), 90 (top & bottom), 92, 93 (top & bottom), 94, 95, 96 (top), 97, 98 (top), 99, 105, 106, 107 (top left), 122, 123, 124;
Images Colour Library, London: 42 (top & bottom), 43 (top), 56, 118, 120, 121 (left & right), 131 (bottom), 132, 139;
Kent Collection, London: 32 (left), 34, 35 (bottom), 74, 79 (top & bottom right);
Mansell Collection, London: 4, 7, 15, 17, 26, 27, 29, 35 (top), 36, 37, 45, 47, 50 (bottom), 53, 70, 71, 76, 78, 86, 87 (right);
Peter Newark's Pictures, Bath: 73 (left), 91, 98 (bottom) (Krylov, Kupryanov & Sokolov *The End*, Tretyakov State Picture Gallery, Moscow), 100 (left), 119 (bottom);
Rex Features, London: 102 (right), 103 (bottom), 107 (right) (Boccon-Gibod/Sipa), 109 (Montreal Gazette/Sipa), 110 (bottom) (Wallis Robert/Sipa), 111 (Rob McElroy/Sipa), 112 (Sipa), 113 (top) (Ozturk/Sipa), 113 (bottom) (F. de Mulder/Sipa), 114 (top) (Chaban al Watan/Sipa), 114 (bottom) (L. Chamussy/Sipa), 115 (Sipa), 116 (L. Delahaye/Sipa), 117 (V. Riviere/Sipa), 125 (top), 126 (T. Haley/Sipa), 127 (Alan Heath), 128 (D. Dancer/Sipa), 129, 130, 133 (Sipa), 135 (Nicolas/Sipa), 136 (top & bottom) (Trippett/Sipa), 137 (top) (Argas/Sipa), 141;
South American Pictures, Woodbridge, Suffolk: 103 (top) (Tony Morrison).